CONVERSATIONS WITH CAPOTE

CONVERSATIONS WITH CAPOTE

BY

Lawrence Grobel

WITH A FOREWORD BY

James A. Michener

NAL BOOKS
NEW AMERICAN LIBRARY
NEW YORK AND SCARBOROUGH, ONTARIO

For information address New American Library

Published simultaneously in Canada by
The New American Library of Canada Limited

NAL BOOKS TRADEMARK REG. U.S. PAT. OFF. AND FOREIGN COUNTRIES
REGISTERED TRADEMARK—MARCA REGISTRADA
HECHO EN HARRISONBURG, VA., U.S.A.

SIGNET, SIGNET CLASSIC, MENTOR, PLUME, MERIDIAN
and NAL BOOKS are published *in the United States*
by New American Library, 1633 Broadway, New York, New York 10019,
in Canada by The New American Library of Canada Limited,
81 Mack Avenue, Scarborough, Ontario M1L 1M8

LIBRARY OF CONGRESS CATALOGING IN PUBLICATION DATA

Grobel, Lawrence.
Conversations with Capote.

Includes index.
1. Capote, Truman, 1924-1984—Interviews.
2. Authors, American—20th century—Interviews.
I. Capote, Truman, 1924–1984. II. Title.
PS3505.A59Z67 1985 813′.54 [B] 84–27324
ISBN 0–453–00494–6

Designed by Julian Hamer

First Printing, February, 1985

1 2 3 4 5 6 7 8 9

PRINTED IN THE UNITED STATES OF AMERICA

for Truman,

who sharpened his pencils
and wasn't afraid

GROBEL: Do you think that remarks can be literature?

CAPOTE: No, but they can be art.

Contents

Foreword
by James A. Michener

Truman Capote was of tremendous importance to writers like me, for he filled a necessary role in American letters, one from which we profited but which we were ill-equipped to perform for ourselves.

England, which has always found a place for the really outrageous eccentric, provided a theater for the naughty Irishman Oscar Wilde, who gave the world, from the salons of London to the mining camps of Colorado, extravagant entertainment.

I never knew the great French artist-poet-actor-poseur Jean Cocteau, but in the years following 1900, when the ineffable Oscar Wilde died, Cocteau became supreme as the visible artist, the man who delighted in the art of *épater la bourgeoisie,* smacking the middle class in the snoot. Extravagant in physical appearance, exhibitionistic by design, flamboyant in action and word, and a superb artist in any medium when he wished to be, he constantly reminded the world that artists were different and that much of their worth stemmed from the fact that they behaved pretty much as they damned well pleased. Cocteau enchanted, bemused, and outraged generations of staid

French and English and German gentlemen, always to the delectation of the watching world and to the enrichment of those who loved either art or boisterous entertainment. Pompous and selfrighteous democracies profit from having men like Jean Cocteau and Oscar Wilde nipping at their heels. They need to be reminded that artists are sometimes outrageously against the grain, that they espouse unpopular causes, that they behave in ways that would be unacceptable to others, and that they can have waspish tongues. I've always had a strong suspicion that such artists help keep society cleaned up, aware, on its toes, and more civilized than it would otherwise be.

In my time in America we have had three such men—Norman Mailer, Gore Vidal, and Truman Capote—and their contributions to our national life have been of inestimable value. Let me illustrate by what happened in the space of five days a few years ago. First, Norman Mailer slugged Gore Vidal in New York, in a public literary brawl which received front-page attention. The next day, John Gardner, a worthy addition to the Terrible Trio, gave an interview to the *Washington Post* in which he stated bluntly that he was the greatest master of English since Chaucer and that worthies like John Milton, Ernest Hemingway, and a flock of other pretenders of such ilk were crocks of something or other. There were so many similar statements that I called the *Post* to verify that Gardner had actually said these things and they assured me: "He said them, and he was sober."

Then, Truman Capote came into our area to speak at a college, but when he lurched onto the stage at eight that evening he was potted and began by abusing the students in rather colorful language. "Why," he wanted to know, "if you want to be writers, aren't you home writing instead of crowding into this hall to listen to an old crock like me?" At that he staggered about, collapsing at the foot of the podium, from where the harassed head of the English department with two helpers lugged his inert body from the stage. End of lecture.

Reading of these dramatic events at the end of one week, I told my wife: "I feel ninety years old at the tail end of a wasted life. I never took part in the main event. I have no claim to call myself a writer." I was secretly jealous of Mailer, Vidal, and Capote. They have borne constant testimony to the fact that they are artists. And they have reminded us that artists often require a special freedom which people in other occupations do not seem to need.

In relation to writers like those who make themselves into public figures, writers like me are much like nonunion members in a work force; we profit from the wage increases gained by the union without being dues-paying members or doing the dirty work of running the strike or policing the ranks. We are freeloaders and we know it.

My association with Truman Capote, whom I revered as a man so opposite to myself, began one day in the offices of Random House when Bennett Cerf ran into where I was working, with a copy of that incredible photograph of the young fawn from the Deep South magnolia plantation reclining languorously on a chaise longue. Beneath the famed photo of the sybarite someone had scrawled a play upon the title of the book which had brought Capote fame: *Other Vices, Other Rooms.*

"Look what some son-of-a-bitch sent me!" Cerf bellowed in his high, agitated voice. But then he could not refrain from laughing. "What you need, Michener, is a photograph like this. An attention-getter."

Occasionally thereafter I would encounter Capote in the editorial offices of Random House, and I was present on that hilarious day when it was revealed that another publisher, so much bigger than Random House that it could risk housing its offices in an unfashionable part of New York, had tried to lure Truman into its fold with promises of vast royalties. Cerf bubbled the news: "Capote was tempted, I have to admit that. They offered him a price we couldn't match. But he finally told them in his high, squeaky voice: 'No young man who aspired to be a serious writer would consent to being published by a house which kept its offices west of Fifth Avenue.'"

Sometime thereafter I fell into Bennett Cerf's doghouse by being seen in the bistros of New York with my longtime friend Leonard Lyons, the *New York Post* columnist who had a penchant for artists, musicians, and writers. Lyons had publicly accused Cerf of filching items from his column for use in the clever anthologies of wit which he, Cerf, was publishing so regularly and successfully. If I wanted to be friends with Lyons, I could not be friends with Cerf, and vice versa. Although Capote and I were Cerf specials, I met Truman only through Lyons; more important, Lyons also introduced me to a stunning would-be starlet-singer-actress-raconteur from the mines of Montana. She had a minimum talent, a maximum beauty, and a rowdy sense of humor. Also, she was six feet, two inches tall, half a head taller than I, a head and a half taller than Truman.

The last point is important, because Truman and

I dated her alternately and she was so delightful to be with that I resented it when she accompanied Truman and not me. They made a stunning pair, this statuesque miner's daughter soaring toward the heavens, this rotund little gnome dancing along beside her. It still grieves me to confess that she liked Truman a good deal more than she did me, partly I think because she knew what a striking pair they made, and this was important to a young woman trying to make her way in New York. She also liked Leonard Lyons, because he used her name in his column rather frequently, and she told me one night: "He'll make me the toast of New York." And for a brief spell he did, for she landed a conspicuous television show, and heads turned whenever she strode in like some Amazonian queen with either Capote or me in tow.

Good girl that she was, she never spoke of Truman to me, or of me to Truman, but we had to be aware of the dual game she was playing, and we did not dislike her for it. I was much smitten by her, as was half of New York that year, and I studied her with care, as well as affection, because she was the first real star—I had promoted her to that category although the rest of the world was rather loath to do so—that I had known. Therefore, when Capote's sensationally good *Breakfast at Tiffany's* appeared and a woman in New York threatened to sue Truman because she claimed that the central character, the ineffable Holly Golightly, had been modeled after her, I, in the goodness of my heart, sat down and penned a letter to Random House defending my fellow author. For reasons which will become apparent, I suppose the letter, which I sent to Donald Klopfer, vice-president of the firm, has been destroyed, but I remember well its contents:

Dear Donald:

I cannot sit by and see your friend and mine, Truman Capote, crucified by the lawsuit which hangs over his head. [A nicely garbled metaphor.] The suit brought by the young woman in New York is patently false because I happen to know without question that Truman patterned Holly Golightly after a wonderful young woman from Montana, and if the suit comes to trial, I shall be willing to so testify.

Jim Michener

Well, the letter had not been in the Random House offices six minutes before Bennett Cerf was on the phone yelling: "Do you have any copies of that crazy letter you sent us?" Before giving me a chance to reply, he added: "Burn them! When I showed Truman your letter he wailed: 'I've been afraid *she's* going to sue, too.'"

It was obvious to me that Capote had fashioned Holly after the sprightly young woman we both liked so much, but she never sued, mainly because she enjoyed the publicity his book had brought her among her circle of café-society friends, who knew the real situation. But after the near-miss with the lawsuits, Truman saw less and less of her, leaving the field to me, and I continued to be stricken by the girl's bubbling charm. I had to withdraw from the competition, however, because of her intense desire to attract attention.

That was the beginning of a desultory acquaintanceship with Capote, who thanked me for the help I had offered, misguided though it was. I met him occasionally at El Morocco, where he squired Marilyn Monroe, who kicked off her shoes while dancing with him (otherwise she too would have been a head taller).

The more I learned about Capote, the more I liked him. Working with a Hollywood producer, I heard that on cross-country trips Truman liked to make the driver take him to the library in some rural county seat and wait while he, Capote, ran inside: "First time it happened, I said nothing. Next time I asked: 'Truman, what in hell are you doing in these libraries?' and he explained with childish delight: 'Checking the card catalogs. In this one Mailer had seven cards. Vidal had eight. But I had eleven.'"

Truman invited me to his great bash at the Waldorf, sensation of that season, but I was in Europe, and I believe I never saw him thereafter. After the debacle in Maryland, where he fell drunk before his student audience, I sent him a note which said: "Hang in there, Kiddo. We need you."

I certainly needed him, for as the years passed I grew ever more grateful to him for playing the role of the genius-clown who reminds the general public that artists are always different and sometimes radically so. My last contact epitomized this belief. I had been working diligently on a manuscript in Random House's New York offices—*slaving away* would be a more appropriate term—when I came out of the offices bleary-eyed to find staring at me from the kiosk in the lobby of the building on East Fiftieth Street the stark white cover of a large Greenwich Village newspaper. It contained no title, only a marvelously debauched photograph of my friend Capote—in Spanish sombrero I think, or perhaps it was a nineteenth-century Toulouse-Lautrec opera hat—leering at me, with four stark lines of type upper left:

I'm an alcoholic
I'm a drug addict

I'm homosexual
I'm a genius

I acknowledged the first three claims, but the last one gave me trouble. In a rather wandering life I have known personally only two geniuses, Tennessee Williams, who used words and human situations more brilliantly than any of us, and Bobby Fischer, the chess champion, who was geared in some wild unique way. Both men found that to be the vessel housing genius was an intolerable condition and each was destroyed by that burden.

Larry Grobel, the conductor of the interviews on which this present book is founded, began his extensive sessions with Capote in New York around the same time he was interviewing me in Florida, and I had the rewarding experience of hearing about them and later his reactions to a fellow writer I had long admired. Grobel said flatly that Capote was a genius; his flow of words, always exactly right, came from no common source.

Grobel's judgment forced me to recalculate my estimates of Capote.

At the time of the publication of *In Cold Blood,* I was working in widely scattered parts of the world, and wherever I went *In Cold Blood* was being translated into the local language with all the impact it had had in English. Critics, readers, other writers were all mesmerized by it, and no other book during my productive years enjoyed such popular and critical acclaim.

I judged at the time that Truman must have earned at least four million dollars from his book and more likely five. His extraordinary wealth allowed him to behave in extraordinary manners.

But it was not for his earnings that I respected him;

it was for his persistence, for the high quality of his work, and for his refusal to be downtrodden. I also relished his mastery of the apt quotation, a skill I lack. And, too, I greatly appreciated the way he applied a sentence I had never heard before, even though others claimed that it was an old classic revived for the telling moment. Capote had been coaching his friend Princess Lee Radziwill, Jackie Kennedy's sister, for a dramatic role in a television play, and she had bombed. Consoling her, Capote said: "The dogs bark and the caravan passes on." As one who lived some years among caravans, I was captivated by the felicity of that remark, whether original with Capote or dredged up by him. I think of it a dozen times a year, and I am grateful to him for bringing it to my attention.

Because a good many young people may read this book, I must clarify one point. I liked Capote despite his troubles, and I treasured him as a fellow writer, but I never enshrined him or Oscar Wilde or Jean Cocteau as the ideal writer. Byron was a Truman Capote of his day; Wordsworth and Goethe were not. Most of the world's fine books are written by ordinary or even drab human beings like Saul Bellow, Anthony Trollope, Gustave Flaubert, Joyce Carol Oates, or Wladislaw Reymont, the Polish Nobel laureat. I obviously enjoy Capote but I would not care to see him replicated endlessly among our youthful aspirants. He should be categorized as a later-day Thomas Chatterton, indubitably brilliant, indubitably incandescent, indubitably doomed.

Is Grobel correct in calling Capote a genius? I'm not sure, because I have stern qualifications for this word, but I would like to throw into the critical hopper two bits of evidence which might support Grobel's contentions.

First, I doubt that any other writer in any language living at the time of the Kansas murders could have written *In Cold Blood* with the severe control that Capote exercised. By that I mean the depiction of an Aeschylean theme without morose moralizing; I mean the choice of precisely the right vocabulary; I mean the management of tension and horror without collapsing into bathos; I mean the telling of a highly personal story—his interaction with two disgusting murderers—without allowing himself to become a central character; I mean also the pioneering of a new style of novel writing. For all these reasons Capote can be praised for having produced a chilling masterpiece. No one but he could have done it at that time, and few could equal it now.

Second, years later I read with enthralled interest excerpts from Capote's last work, the never-to-be-finished *Answered Prayers,* as they appeared in *Esquire* magazine in 1975 and 1976. I had heard for some years that Truman was at work on what he considered his masterpiece and I had developed a more-than-usual interest. A writer constantly hears that some contemporary is at work on the summum bonum opus which will nail down a secure spot in posterity. Mailer is doing such a work. So is James Baldwin. So is Graham Greene. So is Joyce Carol Oates. So is Otto Defore, whom nobody ever heard of, out in Idaho. So are we all.

But here was Capote actually offering samples from his chef d'oeuvre and I was impatient to sample them. Before I finished the second installment my mind was made up and I recorded my judgment in an aide-mémoire to myself:

> A shocking betrayal of confidences, an eating at the table and gossiping in the lavatory. I am familiar with

four of the people T.C. lacerates and I can categorically deny the allegations he makes. A masterly study in pure bitchiness which will close many doors previously opened. Why did he do it? Has he no sense of responsibility or noblesse oblige? A proctologist's view of American society.

But I am sure that if he can bring off the whole, *Answered Prayers* will be the roman à clef of my decade, an American Proust-like work which will be judged to have summarized our epoch. I can visualize graduate students at Harvard in the year 2060 getting their Ph.D.'s in literature by deciphering who Capote's more salacious and infamous characters were and then assessing the justice of his comments. The best of these studies, the one that fixes his reputation, will be titled *Truman Capote and His Age.* Like Toulouse-Lautrec, he will come to represent his period, and he will be treasured for the masterly way he epitomized it.

But only if he can finish his work in high style, only if he incorporates enough leading or relevant figures, only if he masters his subject rather than allowing it to overwhelm him. I hear he's drinking so much and into drugs so heavily that the chances of his making it are slim. What will he have left us then? Some fragments to be covered in footnotes. One hell of a lot of would-be literature is compressed into footnotes.

Because of an unusual combination of circumstances, I was allowed to know Capote tangentially and to assess his performance with some accuracy. I had abiding affection for the man and enormous respect for his talent. I envied the classic manner in which he conducted himself and reveled in his public posturing. His quips were first-class, his best writing of high merit, and his *Cold Blood* exceptional in its mastery.

His going leaves a gap. But I would like my permanent salute to him to be what I told him in my last letter: "Hang in there. We need you."

Austin, Texas
October 1984

Introduction

At noon on Friday, July 16, 1982, I took a taxi from the Drake Hotel to Forty-ninth St. and First Avenue. I was nervous as I walked into La Petite Marmite, just across the street from the UN Plaza, where he lived when he was in the city. "Mr. Capote," I said to the maître d', who led me to a table in the middle of the room. The restaurant was full, but the only person I noticed was Capote, who was sitting there nursing a drink, wearing a blue seersucker jacket over a sweatshirt, his large head perched like a medicine ball upon a short, thick neck.

"Am I late or are you early?" I asked as I sat down next to him.

"I must be early," he said. "I've already ordered my food and I'm having my drink." He put the glass to his lips and took a swallow.

He didn't look the way I expected him to. His face was puffy, his hair thin, his eyes like a crow's. He didn't appear dwarfish or elfin, as he had so often been described, but had an aura of strength and authority.

A waiter came and I ordered a glass of white wine. "Everyone drinks white wine these days," Capote said. "I drink daiquiris."

"Do you drink a lot of them?" I asked.

"No, just two a day."

The waiter handed me a menu and I ordered. Food was the last thing on my mind.

"I've forgotten why we're having this lunch," Capote said.

"To talk about the possibility of doing a television interview," I replied. I had been doing interviews for both *Playboy* magazine and *Playboy* cable and had flown in from California to meet with Capote about a cable interview.

"I despise California. How can you live there?"

"I used to live here," I answered, "but moved to Los Angeles in 1974."

"Why on earth would you do that?" he asked. "You know, it's a scientific fact that if you stay in California you lose one point of your IQ every year. It's quite true, you know."

He was a character, all right. I'd always admired Capote as a writer. I agreed with what Norman Mailer wrote about him in *Advertisements for Myself* when he said, "He is the most perfect writer of my generation, he writes the best sentences word for word, rhythm upon rhythm. I would not have changed two words in *Breakfast at Tiffany's,* which will become a small classic." Also, I remember a professor in college who said that reading Lawrence Durrell was like drinking champagne, but reading Capote was like drinking pure, fresh mountain water. (He also added that Kerouac was like Coca-Cola, which brought a snicker from Capote.)

I wasn't quite sure what to make of Capote the public figure, but any man who could hold hands with Marilyn Monroe, Jacqueline Onassis, and Perry Smith and match wits with the best of his contemporaries was surely someone worth pursuing.

He told me that another cable TV show had asked him to appear but they had made the mistake of sending him a list of the people whom they had already taped. He wasn't impressed. "Especially as they started with Gore Vidal," he laughed.

He then said he didn't want to do any more interviews where he lived because he once allowed Barbara Walters' crew in and they made "such a mess."

I asked him about the cable show he and Joanne Carson were contemplating but he doubted that would ever happen. "They'd have to pay me a lot of money and I hear that money isn't there yet in cable land."

We were interrupted by the appearance of a beaming waiter. "Wait until you see how the chef prepared this for you," he said to Capote.

Truman looked at the fish on his plate and complained, "Oh, this is not the way I wanted it. Oh, but all right, I'll try it."

He studied the fish. "Wellll," Capote said to me, "when would you like to do this?"

"Anytime you'd like," I answered.

He said anytime after the middle of August and then he gave me his two phone numbers, which he asked me to keep secret because he had just had them changed.

I told him that when I was preparing for an interview with Marlon Brando, I found the piece Capote had written for *The New Yorker,* "The Duke in His Domain," to be the most helpful and insightful.

"Yes," he agreed, "but my best celebrity piece is the one I did on Marilyn Monroe."

For the next hour, as he ate his fish and I ate around my crabs, we talked about what was going on in the news and about his writing life. John Hinckley had been judged insane for shooting the President and sentenced to an asylum, which Capote thought was the correct verdict. "He *is* mad, what else?"

Claus von Bulow, however, who had recently been convicted of injecting his wife with a damaging dose of insulin, he considered completely innocent. "I know this for a fact," Capote said. "His wife used to try to teach me how to use a syringe to give myself vitamin B_{12} injections."

I asked why, then, he hadn't appeared at von Bulow's trial.

"Only because I was sure he would be found not guilty. And also because Norman Mailer had made such a spectacle of himself over Jack Abbott, I didn't think it was such a good idea for another writer to do the same. But I will appear when they appeal it."

Although his voice was some octaves above tenor, it wasn't the nasal pitch it seemed when I heard him on television talk shows, which I figured must be his carefully cultivated persona when he's "on."

When I asked him about his writing habits, he said that he got up at four-thirty every morning and was working by five-thirty until twelve-thirty in the afternoon. He said he was a slow writer, going over and over what he wrote, and was currently working on *Answered Prayers* and a book of short stories. He also liked to read his books and said, "Every time I pick up *In Cold Blood* I read it all the way through, as if I didn't write it. It's really quite a perfect book, you know. I wouldn't change anything in it."

"Is it also your favorite book?" I asked.

"No, my favorite book is *The Muses Are Heard.*"

When I asked him who his agent was, he said he didn't have one, just a lawyer. "Why should it cost you twenty percent when the lawyer does the work? Then it's just ten percent. I never had an agent because I sold my first work when I was seventeen and went directly to the publisher. And then I was the youngest person to serve on *The New Yorker.*"

Our conversation switched to the movies and he spoke of the script for his novella *Handcarved Coffins.* The project had been with United Artists, "but there's been a shake-up there and it's now with Twentieth Century-Fox. I read that book about David Begelman, *Indecent Exposure,* and some of the people in that are involved in this, so maybe it isn't so good," he laughed. "I added a reporter to make the script work. I tried to keep myself out of the story as much as possible."

When the bill arrived, Capote insisted on signing for it. He complained about the bursitis in his shoulders and said he had to go to the dentist because his teeth weren't good and he'd had a lot of problems, including correcting what his previous dentist did to his teeth. "He was a crook," he growled as we walked out of the restaurant.

In August I spoke with Capote on the phone to see if we could postpone our interview until October.

"What was it again we were supposed to do?" he asked, his voice sounding as if he were speaking through a strainer. It was the Capote of joke talking, not the same voice as when we had met.

I refreshed his memory and he said, in that strangled voice, "Oh, I just came from one with *60 Minutes* this morning. I just got back. I took a long cold shower, teehee," he giggled. "Hmm, well, I have no objections to doing it. Let me see—I have a lecture to do at the University of California in Berkeley in October."

I suggested that perhaps we could do the interview in Los Angeles when he was on the Coast.

"I hate Los Angeles," he said. "Let me go get my book and see the date. Hold on." When he returned he sounded amazed. "What a miracle, I found it right away—and with the mess that room is in, the way the desk is... Let's see, it's in November I have that lecture. Well, anytime you want to come in October will be fine. Just send me two letters with the date and the time and the place, one to my New York address and the other to my house in Sagaponack. That's S-a-g...hmmm, how *do* you spell it?"

Three weeks later, he called. "How *are* you?" he squeaked. "I got your letter and it will be fine. How is it out there where the waves are pounding?" He was calling from his Sagaponack house, he said, and he was obviously feeling very chipper and friendly.

Our interview was scheduled for Tuesday, October 12, at the Drake Hotel. On Monday I tried calling him but was unable to reach him. On Tuesday morning I tried again and caught him as he was shaving. Yes, he'd be there on time, he said. No, he didn't want a limo to pick him up, he'd take a taxi.

When he arrived I offered him a drink but he refused. After a while, though, as we started taping, he changed his mind and started to drink vodka, straight.

He was cautious at first, but he soon loosened up. He even read his short piece called "Mr. Jones" from *Music for Chameleons,* about a blind, crippled man with a small scarlet star-shaped birthmark on his left cheek who occupied the room next to his when he lived in a Brooklyn rooming house in 1945. Ten years later, in a subway car in Moscow, Capote saw the man sitting opposite him—only he wasn't blind or crippled, but he had that same distinctive birthmark. When he finished reading, he closed the book with some satisfaction and drawled, "So much for Russian spies."

Since the interview went so well—and since I knew we'd be using only about eight minutes of it on the air—I asked Truman when we had finished if he wouldn't mind continuing our talk for some future project. I didn't have anything in mind then, other than the thought that I was recording history and that he was a wonderfully entertaining talker. And, also, I had so overprepared for this interview that I had hundreds of questions left to ask.

"I don't mind," he said, suggesting that I might consider coming to Berkeley in November.

But Berkeley didn't work out. When I called him about it, he said he was flying in only for the day and had to return to the East immediately. He also asked if I would eliminate two things from our talk: something he had said about Thomas Thompson, who had recently died, and one particular thing he had called Jacqueline Onassis. "You can leave everything else, just take that out."

He said he had been working hard, "slavering, I call it," and complained about the heat in New York, which was "over eighty."

I told him about a survey taken of the reading habits of teenagers in Cleveland and the books they would like their parents to read. The number-one choice was *In Cold Blood.* Other books mentioned were *Go Ask Alice, I'm O.K., You're O.K., Of Mice and Men,* and *The Old Man and the Sea.*

"I dislike *The Old Man and the Sea* intensely," Capote said, "but the others you can keep."

* * *

I spoke with him again on December 2 and his first words were, "Oh, how's our movie coming?"

I asked him if he had any pictures of himself which we might be able to use and he said he had one when he was sixteen, in high school, which was "rather nice, very casual. And Carl Van Vechten took a picture when I was first at *The New Yorker* which is very striking. It's in his book of photographs which came out about three years ago. He's dead now. So's his wife. Actually, there are two pictures that are turning points in my life. That one when I was sixteen and just quit high school and one by Cartier-Bresson when I was eighteen."

"Is that the one printed on the back of the twentieth-anniversary edition of *Other Voices, Other Rooms?*" I asked.

"Yes, that's the one. The difference between the two pictures is absolutely staggering. They're both quite extraordinary."

But something was wrong. He sounded very tired and frail. I asked him how he was and he said, "Since I saw you, the very next day, I've been having these stomach pains. When I did that lecture in Berkeley, I got this incredible pain. I had a doctor giving me Demerol, it was an agonizing experience. And when I got back, I went to the hospital every day for examinations. I had a stomachache from something else and they were doing all these tests and it was by accident that they found a very large and dangerous polyp in my colon. They put this white, gooey stuff inside my stomach and X-rayed me from top to bottom. I've been in unbelievable pain. I'm going to the hospital on Sunday. It'll be all right, it won't grow back. I tell you, you'd best get yourself fully X-rayed, from top to bottom."

"Have you been able to work at all?"

"I've been too sick to do anything. I'm just trying to take it easy."

"Are you able to eat?"

"I can't. If I eat anything it gives me a terrific stomachache. I'm not supposed to drink milk, either," he said with that laugh of his. "It's just weird. Hopefully, I'll lose some weight."

"What hospital are you going to?"

"Mount Sinai. But please, don't tell anybody about this."

I called him again the next day and when he asked me, "How is it out there in dear old deathland?" I knew he must be feeling better.

"You know," he quipped, "I've told you, you're losing your IQ minute by minute out there, second by second, tick tick tick tick. Why don't you move back to New York?"

"I've got too much family there," I joked.

"Well, there's a way to avoid that," he said with a laugh. "There's a lovely story in the paper today about a thirteen-year-old boy who took a .45 magnum and shot his mother to death in her stomach. When asked why he did it, he said, 'Because she wanted me to go to school.' You see, we have jolly things going on here!"

"Well," I laughed, "we've got newspapers filled with stories like that out here, so I'm not missing anything."

"Oh, that pitiful paper you've got out there," he said, referring to the *Herald Examiner*. "Golly Moses, they should make Patty Hearst the editor. She'd jazz it up. Give the inside story of the police department!"

Then he asked me if I had seen *The Ladies' Home Journal,* which had published the Christmas story about his father. "You see," he said, "it was the other side of the coin. In 'A Christmas Memory,' I never mentioned my father. I never mentioned him *ever* in my writing. He died last year. Random House is going to publish it in one of those strip cover books, making a real pretty one next year. *Ladies' Home Journal* made a very pretty little edition of it to send to all of their advertisers. But magazines... *Playboy*'s the only one that's entirely honest.

"I got a letter, you wouldn't believe, from an editor at *McCall's,* for giving the story to *Ladies' Home Journal.* He said he had a letter he had sent to me asking me to do one for their Christmas issue. I don't remember getting that letter. He was absolutely violent! You see, I was very affected by my father's death. I didn't think I was, until I started writing about him. I let this writer read it and he's a friend of the *Ladies' Home Journal*'s editor. She drove to the country to see me, saying she must publish it. She was very sweet. I said, 'All right.' Well, wow! I mean, you'd think like I ought to be in Creedmore, the way this *McCall's* editor wrote! Oh dear, honest God, the nerve!"

Then I asked him how he was feeling, which was the real reason for my call. I told him I had talked with someone who had a polyp in the colon and it was treated with sulfur and it wasn't too bad. But he said, "Two things have to be done at the same time. The polyp and something called diverticulitis, do you know what that is? Lyndon Johnson had it, he was so proud of showing off his scar."

He changed the subject to *Vanity Fair,* a publication he had recently had a falling-out with. "But I'm so glad to be rid of *Vanity Fair,* I can't tell you. I already feel as if I had my operation."

We both laughed and he asked if I'd seen the picture of him in *Newsweek,* "with the children. It's delightful, it's so sweet—I should close on that." He laughed again and I wished him both calm and luck.

A few weeks later I called to find out how things went. "Let's not talk about my recuperating," he said, "since it's not going so well."

I said that I'd like to fly in to see him and continue our interview at the end of January. Fine, he said, he'd be there.

But when I went to New York I found out that he had gone to Switzerland, where, I assumed, he could better recuperate.

I didn't speak to him again until May 1983. I had heard that he had been hospitalized after having an epileptic seizure. When I finally reached him on the phone, we had a terrible connection. His choppy voice sounded as if it was going through a blender, with words being cut off. I told him I was having a hard time hearing him and he said that was because he'd been having such a rough time lately.

"It hasn't been easy for you these last months," I said.

"It hasn't been easy since 1924, when I was born," he laughed. Then he told me that he had had an accident and almost cut his right hand in half. I tried to ask him more about it, but I couldn't make out his answer.

When he asked me about California, I granted that I had probably lost two IQ points since we last talked.

"Yes, that's probably true. You should stay home, with all your doors locked, don't go out."

"That's what I tell my parents, who live on Long Island," I joked.

"Poor them," he laughed. "So many murders, every two minutes, occur there."

* * *

Mid-May, I was back in New York and I drove out to Bridgehampton in a pouring rain to meet Truman at Bobby Van's, a restaurant located on the main street of the small town. He was there when I arrived a few minutes before noon. He was wearing a red sweatshirt and he looked older. Wisps of white hair fell down the back of his huge head, very thin blond hair came to a V on top. The nails on his short stubby fingers were long and he was drinking already, sitting alone at a corner round table which could seat eight. There was a setting right next to him, but I took a different seat. He noticed immediately and pushed away the chair next to him and said, "Let's move this so that our words will have room to *fly* across the table." I had hoped to go to his home in Sagaponack, but he said it was too messy.

"I don't mind," I said.

"Yes, but I do." He explained that his lover, Jack Dunphy, was there, putting the finishing touches on a book he had written about the New York City Ballet tour. He told me how Dunphy had been married to a dancer and George Balanchine and this other director of the New York City Ballet had looked at Jack and asked *him* to try out. Dunphy did, and although he didn't know how to dance, they raved about him and he wound up in the company.

"Don't you have two houses next to each other?" I asked.

Yes, he did, but he *still* didn't want to go there.

"Do you know someplace we can go where it's quiet?" I asked. I was worried about the restaurant filling up for lunch. Truman was difficult enough to hear when it was quiet.

"Oh," he intoned with a raised devilish look, "I know someplace where we can go," and he hummed a laugh.

"Okay," I said, "we'll obviously be staying here."

We started to talk about writing and he spoke of Henry James's worst novel, *The Golden Bowl,* and how it had been "totally dictated." I took out my little Sony and put it on the table. For the next five and a half hours he'd move it a bit away and I'd push it a bit closer, hoping to get his words, which he often swallowed. This time I was more aware of his extraordinary, intense eyes, especially when he looked right at me. I also found myself staring more at his mouth with that lolling serpent's tongue. I felt as though I might be sucked in when he leaned forward. I half-expected that tongue to lash out froglike and whip around my neck.

I gave him an eight-by-ten photograph Harvey Wang had made of him when we were at the Drake. It's a strong head shot, showing a determined-faced Capote who looks like he's got much on his mind. Truman stared at it for a while and pronounced it "quite good," although, he said, he wouldn't want to send it as a Christmas card. Then he laughed and said, "It's the kind of picture you send to an old lover and say, 'It's a good thing you left or look what you would have ended up with.'"

I had also brought a copy of *The Muses Are Heard* and the coffee-table-sized *Observations*—a book he did in collaboration with photographer Richard Avedon—a book he said he had recently tried to buy, but it was selling for six hundred dollars. He picked up *The Muses Are Heard* and wrote an amusing dialogue exchange inside, then read it to himself and commented, "Hmm, this is pretty good, maybe I should publish it." Then he looked through the other book and held up the picture Avedon shot of him, saying to Barbara, our waitress, "Would you like to see a picture of me?"

Barbara looked at the young Truman, with those same soulful, intense eyes, and said, "Oh, Truman, is that you? You look so handsome."

"Hmm, yes, that is a nice photo," Truman agreed.

He was in droll form that day, making acerbic comments about almost everyone I brought up. After a few drinks, I excused myself to go to the bathroom.

"You mean you're not the brave macho"—he pronounced it with a hard *k, mako*—"journalist who doesn't move until he's got the story? You're a human being who has to pee just like everybody else?"

When I returned, I noticed he was working on his fourth "double" (he drank Stolichnaya vodka with two ice cubes and grapefruit juice on the side) and I asked him what kind of car he had. He said he had three: a Mustang, which was in its original condition and which he preferred to drive; a Jaguar; and a four-year-old Rolls-Royce Corniche. "I kept them in the city where I live but it got so expensive to keep them there and then the Rolls got four dents while it was just parked there so I complained to the garage, but they wouldn't fire the man who caused the dents so I took all my cars out of there and brought them here."

It was dark out when I remembered I had a dinner engagement in the city. "Are you in a rush?" Truman asked. "Oh well, let's then have one more drink and you can go. I'll stay here because I'm meeting someone at six."

* * *

In June, James Michener was in Los Angeles and I went to see him. We talked of Mailer and Capote and he said, "You sure can't find three more different writers than Norman, Capote, and me."

I told him how I had been seeing Capote periodically now for about a year and Michener recalled the remark he had once made to me about *Answered Prayers* being the most remembered book of our times, if Capote ever finished it. "I still think that, you know," he said, "The roman à clef is a fascinating world of its own, where you can read such a novel and trace back to who was who. We need Truman among us. He's necessary for us, because of what he represents. I remember when I was in Japan after the war and there was this French homosexual who always dressed in red velvet and was quite outlandish. Still, he was hauled out for every social function, because you knew he represented culture, it didn't matter what he did. And Truman is that for us."

At the end of June I spoke to Capote in Sagaponack. Once again, we had a bad connection, made much worse by his speech. He said he was working on a piece about Tennessee Williams for *Playboy,* which he was calling "Death of a Stranger." He also said he had to have another operation, "the same thing as last time, only the doctor hasn't made up his mind when. It's been so hot here."

"Why not come out to L.A.?" I chided. "I'll be happy to put you up."

"I would rather commit suicide on the Long Island Expressway than even consider such a thing," he said, laughing his Capote laugh.

* * *

I didn't get back to New York until October. Naturally, I called Capote and drove out to Bridgehampton to continue our talks at Bobby Van's. This time he was late and I waited for him at the bar, where a picture of him, James Jones, Willie Morris, and John Knowles hangs. When he showed up, we sat at a table next to eight yakking women. I had brought a different tape recorder with individual mikes, and when I started to set up, he complained that I shouldn't start so quickly, he had just arrived. But I wanted to get set so when we started talking, I wouldn't have to fumble around.

"I thought I told you to get rid of that stuff," Truman said about the tape recorder.

"I don't have your total recall," I said.

He told me about the stabbing chest pains he'd been having and about the ordeal with the judge who got so angry when he appeared in court on a drunken-driving charge wearing sandals and shorts that he refused to try the case at that time. He seemed healthier than he had in the past and he was playful when we finished.

"I'm going to let you drive me home," he said, "but I'm not going to let you in." But first he asked me to stop at a liquor store, which was closed. He tapped at the window and the owner came and, recognizing who it was, sold him a bottle of vodka. We drove along the stark, flat land that makes up the end of Long Island, and it reminded me of the Kansas plains Capote so well described in *In Cold Blood.* At Daniel's Lane, we turned and drove awhile, until we came to the two small cottages where he and Jack Dunphy lived. He pointed out the garage between the two houses where his cars were, and complained again about what a shambles his house was in.

"Now, I want you to wait, with your lights on," he instructed, "until I get into the house."

I waited, my car running, the headlights providing a path of light to his door. I watched as this rotund man with his bottle of vodka tucked under his arm entered his house, and then I saw him put the bottle down and open the refrigerator—this small brilliant man in the lonely wooden house far out on the edge of Long Island.

In May 1984 I went to a movie theater in Hollywood to see two Christopher Isherwood films, *Rage in Heaven* and *The Loved One.* As I sat in my seat, Isherwood and Don Bachardy entered and sat in front of me. I once took a course at UCLA with Isherwood and I started to speak to him. It wasn't long before Capote's name came up and Isherwood told the story of how strong Truman was, having once beaten Humphrey Bogart in an arm wrestle.

He was sorry to hear about Capote's epilepsy, "but people can live a long life with epilepsy. Truman, you know, was a very good swimmer. He was always small but, as the expression goes, he's built like a brick shithouse." He laughed. "Yes, I like him very much."

In June I spoke with Capote on the phone, but could barely understand him.

"Whatever happened to the film we made?" he asked.

"It ran a long time ago," I said. "Didn't I send you a copy?"

"I don't know. I don't really care," he sighed.

I told him that I had finally finished a first draft of the novel I had been working on and he asked me who was going to publish it. This time it was my turn to say, "I don't know."

He offered encouragement and then asked me something, but I couldn't make out what he had said. I answered no. He asked me something else and again I couldn't understand him. I answered: I think so. It had always been a struggle to speak with him over the phone, but this time was by far the worst. I assumed he must be under a lot of medication. And who knows how many "doubles" from Bobby Van's?

"Have you been working?" I asked.

Yes, he had.

"How are you feeling?"

Fine, just fine.

"I found a first edition of *Local Color,*" I said. "It's quite a nice-looking book."

He laughed. "I'll see you when you come in," he said.

"Of course you will," I said. There was nothing more to say. I was just glad to have made contact.

It was our last conversation. Two months later, Truman flew out to "deathland" to stay with his friend Joanne Carson. He was helping her plan the party she wanted to give for him at the end of September. He would have been sixty years old.

1

Fame, Notoriety, and Genius

"I don't know anybody who gets
as much publicity as I do
for doing nothing."

"In his teens," wrote Brendan Gill in his book *Here at The New Yorker*, "Capote served for a time as an office boy on *The New Yorker*. He was a tiny, round-faced, slender creature, as exotic as an osprey. . . . Capote dressed with an eccentricity that wasn't to become a commonplace among the young for another twenty-five years; I recall him sweeping through the corridors of the magazine in a black opera cape, his long golden hair falling to his shoulders: an apparition that put one in mind of Oscar Wilde in Nevada, in his velvets and lilies."

Norman Mailer, in a piece he wrote for *Esquire* about television, called "Of a Small and Modest Malignancy," described the first time he met Capote—on the drive out to Newark, where they, along with Dorothy Parker, were to appear on David Susskind's *Open End*.

"Truman did much complaining on the trip out," Mailer wrote. "'I didn't want to do this show,' he said in a dry little voice that seemed to issue from an unmoistened reed in his nostril. 'I told Bennett Cerf it was a mistake, but Bennett thinks television is going to be very important for selling our books.'"

As the show progressed, Mailer sketched in the details of how well he felt he was doing until the discussion turned to the merits of Jack Kerouac, whom Capote detested. "As Mailer grew benign," Mailer wrote of himself, "Capote grew precise. He rose at last to his own peroration and invoked the difficulties of the literary craft in contrast to Mr. Kerouac's undisciplined methods of work. Finally, in a tone of fearless and absolute severity, Capote said: 'It is not writing. It is only typing.'

"'I agree,' said Dorothy Parker in a hoarse voice.

"'Well, I don't,' said Mailer, only to give a limp defense. He was empty of vast indignation at this dreadful put-down of Kerouac."

On the drive home, Capote kept praising Mailer's performance and putting his own down. They went to eat at El Morocco and Capote's spirits revived. Mailer also discovered Capote's charm that night, understanding how he had become "the in-house author of the most important hostesses in New York." What Mailer felt was envy. Still, it was a grand evening, according to Mailer, "and at the end, Truman announced they would be great friends forever."

But the next day, praise of Mailer's performance was not forthcoming and he took a walk. A friend stopped him and said, "It is not writing, it is *only* typing," and laughed. Another said: "Truman; too much!" A third asked, "Could you get me to meet Capote?"

Finally, in frustration, Mailer called *Open End* and asked to see the show. What he saw gave him a new understanding of the medium. "Capote did not look small on the show, but large! His face, in fact, was extraordinary, that young-old face, still pretty and with such promise of oncoming ugliness; that voice, so full of snide rustlings and unforgiving nasalities; it was a voice to knock New York on its ear. The voice had survived; it spoke of horrors seen and passed over; it told of judgments that would be merciless."

Acknowledging the impact Capote had made, Mailer felt defeated. And the next time he saw Capote, he "had a new assurance to put on top of the old one . . . a difference in Truman's idea of himself had begun to appear. That personality he had presented, with all his early bravado, to a most special part of the world, was, it seemed, going to be accepted by all the world."

It certainly was.

You've always thought of yourself as a two-headed calf. In other words, in your own eyes, you felt that you were different, a freak. Is that the way you really feel about yourself?

I said it about myself but I really meant it about all artists. I think that all artists are two-headed calves.

Being an artist separates you from things in general. One's mind is working at a faster, more sensitive, more rapid, eye-batting level than most people's. Most people, let's say, have ten perceptions per minute, whereas an artist has about sixty or seventy perceptions per minute.

Is that constant or are you able to turn off—or tone down—these perceptions?

I think that that's honestly the reason why so many writers drink or take pills or whatever: to calm themselves down, to quiet this continuous, rapid-running machine. I know that's why Tennessee Williams did. He had to take sedatives and drinks like that because he had one of the most rapid-running, perceptive minds. He didn't sleep very well.

And you?

I have a lot of problems sleeping.

You wrote about those problems in the last piece in Music for Chameleons, *"Nocturnal Turnings." It became famous for the lines near the end, when you wrote, "I'm not a saint yet. I'm an alcoholic. I'm a drug addict. I'm homosexual. I'm a genius." Where are you in relation to what you wrote then?*

Well, I'm not an alcoholic. I had an alcoholic period at one time. I'm not a drug addict at all. I had a slight period of taking pills at one time. I just put that in there as a sort of joke, but when it's taken out of context, which a lot of the reviewers did, then it comes out sounding quite strange.

Were you joking about being a genius?

I sort of meant it two ways. I half meant it and half meant it as a joke.

What is genius to you?

Being able to do something in an exceptional way that nobody else can do.

Proust defined genius as: originality, charm, finesse, strength. He said genius consists in the power to reflect and not in the intrinsic value of the thing reflected. Do you agree?

Yes. In the sense that I don't think that what an artist uses as his subject is as important as *how* he uses it. That's what makes the difference between a very fine talent and somebody who just has a talent. A very fine artist can take something quite ordinary and, through sheer artistry and willpower, turn it into a work of art.

For instance?

Actors seem to do it more often than, say, musicians. Although certain singers can take a very bad song and, simply because of a tremendous sense of style and power, turn it into an amazing thing, like Billie Holiday. Billie Holiday scarcely in her whole life ever sang a really good song, but she took these perfectly mediocre songs and turned them into amazing powerhouses of style and artistry. There was somebody who could take an apple out of a basket and turn it into a work of art no matter how rotten the apple was. Because she had style. Lee Wiley was another great stylist. She never got the credit she deserved. It's really from Lee Wiley and Billie Holiday that Frank Sinatra learned everything about reading a lyric. He's a good lyric reader.

What about writers? Who among your contemporaries would you consider a genius?

Flannery O'Connor had a certain genius. I don't think John Updike has, or Norman Mailer or William Styron, all of whom are talented, but they don't exceed themselves in any way. Norman Mailer thinks William Burroughs is a genius, which I think is ludicrous beyond words. I don't think William Burroughs has an ounce of talent.

James Michener once told me the only two people he's known whom he ever considered geniuses were Bobby Fischer and Tennessee Williams.

It's entirely possible Bobby Fischer *is* a genius. Tennessee, at a certain point in his life, was, but toward the end he spread himself out and became more interested in painting than in writing.

You've been criticized for spreading your own interests between your art and the pursuit of celebrity. The late Thomas Thompson called you a creature in the celebrity zoo. He felt you seriously damaged your career by succumbing to celebrity.

He seriously damaged his career by ever publishing a book.

Nevertheless, regarding your own celebrity, has it affected you?

No, of course not.

In Here at The New Yorker, *Brendan Gill said that you promote yourself as other people promote lipstick or baby powder. Any truth there?*

No. Not in my opinion.

Still, you seem to get into the papers more for yourself than for your work.

Isn't that true of anybody? I mean, I *am* a personality. I read in *The New York Times* about how difficult the publicity thing was for books and writers. They ended the article by saying that publishers couldn't get their writers on television except those that had to do with exercises and health. But the average novelist that has written a literary book of any kind, they didn't consider it. "And, of course, this doesn't apply to Truman Capote, because they consider him a personality as well as a novelist." (*Laughs.*) I've had enough publicity to last an army of super rats. I don't know anybody who gets as much publicity as I do for doing nothing.

Would you prefer being less well-known so you could be more of a fly-on-the-wall?

It's long past the time I can do anything about it. I mean, it all started when I was sixteen. I had a whole article done about me in *Life* magazine, a prodigy writer, you know. From that point on it's been a foregone conclusion. If you're a celebrity, you're a celebrity. That's the end of the question. You can't change that.

Would you agree with Proust that our social personality is the creation of others?

Not mine! (*Laughs.*)

Certainly not your voice. Mailer called it "a voice to knock New York on its ear."

Oh, that's just because it knocked him on his ear when I did him in on this television program.

Still, many people have described your voice. How do you feel about that?

I don't know. I can always tell when an interview with

me is going to be slightly hostile because, in the very first paragraph, whoever's writing the interview right away mentions something about my voice. From that moment on I know that, hmmmm, just hold on here, we're going to find some rainy clouds ahead. (*Laughs.*) The one thing I don't understand is that people have written that I have a lisp. Well, I've made nine records of my stories for Columbia and for RCA Records and if you can find this lisp on the records, I'll give you a hundred thousand dollars!

In Breakfast at Tiffany's, *you wrote, "The average personality reshapes frequently." Holly Golightly's did not. Does yours?*

Not frequently as a personality. My attitude changes shape over a period of time. I feel much more distant and different now than I ever have before.

You've said that you felt very distant from the writer who wrote your first novel, Other Voices, Other Rooms. *That's what really established you as a personality, isn't it?*

Yes. The book itself got very good reviews. It was a best-seller. But oddly, the photograph of me on the back of the book aroused a great deal of controversy. *Time* magazine didn't appear for twelve issues in a row without having some vicious thing to say about me. All kinds of really dreadful things were written and said.

All because of that picture?

Yes.

Did you select that picture?

I had nothing to do with it. It was just a photograph taken by a friend of mine that wasn't intended to be on anything. They wanted a picture of me and I was in California, so I told my editor, Mr. Linscott, who's now dead, to go to my apartment and in the desk drawer there were quite a few photographs of me, just pick one that he liked. A lot of people have taken pictures of me for different magazines, but that particular picture wasn't taken for anything. And he picked that picture out. I didn't see anything wrong with it. Nothing occurred to me about it until it was published. They used it rather largely in their ads and it created all of this great stir of controversy. Other publishers told Bennett Cerf, who was the head of Random House, that it was outrageous of him to publish a photograph like that. But the picture's perfectly harmless. It's just me lying on the sofa looking at the camera. But I guess it assumes that I'm lying on the sofa and more or less beckoning somebody to climb on top of me.

One thing about all of that was that it increased your love life.

(Warily.) Ye-ess.

Do you credit that to the notoriety caused by the picture or to the book itself?

Oh, I think it was the fame. I mean, people are very interested and curious about it.

How did fame affect you? You were awfully young at the time.

Mm-hmmm. I have very mixed feelings about it. I can't say that it made me entirely happy because it certainly didn't. It caused me a lot of trouble and changed my life completely. Most people who become suddenly famous overnight will find that they lose practically eighty percent of their friends. Your old friends just can't stand it for some reason. I've seen it happen over and over, and people to whom it's happened agree with me. I had a lot of friends and I lost them overnight.

When did you become indifferent toward fame? When were you able to ignore it?

Oh, pretty soon. It took about two years.

Fame, of course, brought you a readership. How many people in America do you think have read something you've written?

I think everybody who's been to school in the last twenty years and has taken an English course has to have read at least one story of mine because they're used in almost all English courses. So many books that are done for schools print that story of mine, "A Christmas Memory." And anybody in any kind of journalist course has read *In Cold Blood.* It's one of the books most used in journalism and in English classes because many teachers have one book that they assign that they can be sure the students will read (*laughs*), once they start reading it, just because of the pure narrative drive. But the real reason that they use it is because it's well written, in their opinion, and it's highly usable for teaching. At the same time, it's something that they can be sure that even the most reluctant student will drag himself through. (*Laughs.*) At least fifteen million people in this country have read *In Cold Blood* because I've sold almost that many copies of the book. So that assumes that only one person read the book, but usually it's more than that.

What about reviews—can they get to you?

On the whole, I'm unfazed by them. I never read unpleasant things about myself. Not that it really bothers me, but why should I get annoyed with it? The only time I ever remember being really angry at something was in the *New Republic.* It wasn't really a review, it was an article by Stanley Kauffmann, who, of course, is next door to John Simon as a super jerk. He wrote an all-out onslaught attack on me which was very unfair. I was annoyed by that, but that's the only time I can remember being really annoyed. Oh, yes, I can remember another. You know the O. Henry Memorial Awards? Well, one year I won first prize. I won it a couple of times, but anyway, this one year I won first prize and *The New York Times* reviewed the entire book, all of the stories in it, and it didn't mention my story at all, even though I had won first prize. And I thought, this is malice beyond malice. Especially since it happened to have been written by the boyfriend of a current boyfriend of mine (*laughs*), which made me even angrier.

Did you consider writing a letter to the editor in protest?

No, I never write letters to the editor about anything. No matter what's written or printed about me, I never write or complain. I do truly believe in: Never explain and never complain.

Two people whose opinions you respected felt that you were too sensitive to criticism: Camus and Willa Cather.

Yeah, they said it, but it isn't true. They got that idea because I used to complain about things that were written about me. Camus was my editor at Gallimard in France until he died. Willa Cather was a great friend of mine. I used to complain to them about what annoyed me, which gave them the idea that I was overly sensitive to it but, in fact, I really wasn't. I was just talking about the untruthfulness of certain things.

You feel, then, that you have a fairly thick skin?

I'd better! (*Laughs.*)

Of all that has been written about you, what publicity has disturbed you the most?

The time that that thing happened at the University of Maryland.

Where you were allegedly drunk and you fell off the podium?

Well, I didn't fall off the podium. I *walked* off the stage. I was terribly upset by something that happened just the day before—like, the most upset I've ever been in my life.

I was beside myself. And I just began drinking vodka and just couldn't stop—up until the very moment that I walked on the stage and was introduced by the president of the university. Suddenly, something happened as I started the program and in this rage that I had going it threw me into an absolute fury. I slammed the book down on the stage and walked off, saying terrible things. Unfortunately for me, there was a whole lot of press there from Baltimore and Washington, and the *Washington Post*—owned by my dear friend Mrs. Graham—ran my picture throwing the fit on the front page the next day. It got a terrible amount of publicity in all the newsmagazines and it upset me a lot. Because I was *already* upset... and then to have this awful thing happen to me in front of five thousand people... it was all too much.

You also received a great deal of coverage for the Black and White Ball you threw in the sixties, where everyone had to wear a mask—which was a wonderful social comment about who people are, think they are, and are not. Did they all go along?

They certainly did. And they weren't allowed to take their masks off until midnight—so nobody really knew who anybody was! (*Laughs.*)

Were people aware of what you were trying to do?

Well, the whole party was a statement of art. It was really very beautiful, really was spectacular to see—what I had done with it visually, not just who was there, because I had everybody there.

Did anyone turn you down?

No. Far from it! I made about a million and a half lasting enemies over that party.

Not everyone can get an invitation to the party of the decade. How much did it cost you?

It cost about $155,000. And I didn't get a single tax

deduction from it, either. Lots of people thought I got a big tax deduction, but I didn't get one dime or nickle out of it.

You did get something from an autograph seeker in a Key West bar—an amusing story? Could you relate it?

It was in a bar in Key West and it was very, very crowded. I was sitting there with Tennessee. And this woman came over to this table where we were sitting and she had on a little pull-up shirt and she pulled up her shirt and handed me an eyebrow pencil. And she said, "I want you to autograph my navel." I said, "What?" And she said, "Just write it like you would the numerals around a clock." I said, "Oh no, forget that." And Tennessee said, "Oh, now, go on, go ahead." So I wrote my name: T-R-U-M-A-N C-A-P-O-T-E. Right around her navel, like a clock. This had caused a certain silence in this room. She went back to her table and her husband was in a rage. He was drunk as all get-out, and he got up from the table and came over and he had the eyebrow pencil in his hand. He looked at me with this infinite hatred, handed me the eyebrow pencil, unzipped his fly, and hauled out his equipment. By this point there was a dead, total silence in the whole bar. Everybody was looking. And he said, "Since you're autographing everything, how'd you like to autograph *this*?" There was a pause... and I said, "Well, I don't know if I can autograph it, but perhaps I could initial it."

2

Growing Up

"I started to write when I was eight years old. I mean, really seriously. So seriously that I dared never mention it to anybody."

"I was born in New Orleans, an only child," Capote wrote in the foreword to the twentieth-anniversary edition of his first novel, *Other Voices, Other Rooms*; "my parents were divorced when I was four years old. It was a complicated divorce with much bitterness on either side, which is the main reason why I spent most of my childhood wandering among the homes of relatives in Louisiana, Mississippi, and rural Alabama (off and on, I attended schools in New York City and Connecticut.) The reading I did on my own was of greater importance than my official education, which was a waste and ended when I was seventeen."

The same year he wrote that foreword he told Eric Norden in a *Playboy* interview that the book was a "prose poem in which I have taken my own emotional problems and transformed them into pyschological symbols. Every one of the characters represented some aspect of myself. Do you remember the young boy who goes to a crumbling mansion in search of his father and finds an old man who is crippled and can't speak and can communicate only by bouncing red tennis balls down the stairs? . . . This represented my search for my own father, whom I seldom saw, and the fact that the old man is crippled and mute was my way of transferring my own inability to communicate with my father; I was not only the boy in the story but also the old man. So the central theme of the book was my search for my father—a father who, in the deepest sense, was nonexistent."

He went on to say that so much of his earlier work was written in a fantastic vein because he was attempting to escape "from the realities of my own troubled life, which wasn't easy. My underlying motivation was a quest for some sense of serenity, some particular kind of affection that I needed and wanted . . . I never felt I belonged anywhere."

GROWING UP

Your main character, Joel, in Other Voices, Other Rooms, *wanted most to be loved. Was that what you also wanted most when you were a boy?*

I had a very difficult childhood. I was very much loved by this elderly woman who was a cousin of mine. I was loved by my mother and father, but I never saw them. My mother was sixteen years old when she was married. I was born when she was seventeen. She left my father to go to college and she went from college on to a career and then she married a very rich man and I went on living in the South with my mother's family. I very seldom saw my father, who lived in New Orleans. Except for my cousins and relatives, there was a great absence of love in my childhood. . . . But I made up for it. (*Laughs.*)

Your father's name was Archulus Persons and yours was Truman Persons until you took your stepfather Joe's last name, correct?

Yes, Truman Streckfus Persons. I could have kept that if it hadn't been for T. S. Eliot. I could have called myself T. S. Persons.

Was your mother an alcoholic?

Yes.

Did she sometimes leave you locked alone in hotel rooms when you were still a toddler?

Yes.... It was a certain period in my life. I was only about two years old, but I was very aware of being locked in this hotel room. My mother was a very young girl. We were living in this hotel in New Orleans. She had no one to leave me with. She had no money and she had nothing to do with my father. She would leave me locked in this hotel room when she went out in the evening with her beaus and I would become hysterical because I couldn't get out of this room.

When you were with your mother then, did you find yourself clinging to her more, wanting her to love you more, be with you and not lock you up like that?

I can't remember anything about that whole period except things like that. Because very soon after that I was separated from her and went to live with a family in Alabama that I wrote all those stories about.

Your mother eventually committed suicide?

Yes.

Did you have any inkling that this might happen?

No.

Where were you when it did?

I was in Europe making a movie called *Beat the Devil* with John Huston and Humphrey Bogart. I wrote the script for it. I'd been in Europe for a year, so I'd only spoken to her on the telephone.

Is it still a painful subject? Did it really hit you hard when you found out?

I was very upset, yes.

Do you think about her often since then?

Yes.

What's the memory you have of her?

She was very intelligent. She was very, very beautiful. She had this complex and she killed herself because she felt her husband was being unfaithful to her and was having affairs which, in fact, he was. But I must say he wasn't all *that* obvious about it. But anyway, it just drove her around the bend.

This was Joe?

Yes. He was also a chronic gambler and his gambling basically ruined my mother's life. I hate gambling.

Do you resent Joe?

No. Since my mother died, he's been married twice. I don't see him at all. It's not that I have something against him. I disliked his first wife after my mother died. She died, too. But the third one was a very strange woman. I just couldn't stand her. She kept calling me on the telephone all the time. I think she only married him to talk to me. I mean that literally. One day I told him, "I don't want to hear from your wife anymore. I really don't like her."

And you haven't heard from him either, since then?

Virtually. But what are you going to do? Did you read this horrendous book written by this crazy aunt of mine? I mean, that book was a lie from the word go—one of the absolutely stupidest things imaginable. That's pretty shocking, I think.

The book, Truman Capote, *by Marie Rudisill, is subtitled "The Story of His Bizarre and Exotic Boyhood by an Aunt Who Helped Raise Him." Was it really* all *a lie?*

All a lie. I promise you. It was mostly a complete lie about me. I never had any relationship with this aunt at all. I scarcely even have the vaguest memory of her. I never had any conversations with her at all. It's completely insane. Well, there have to be thirty true words in it because of the names of people. But it's the most ridiculous book. I couldn't care less, but I feel sort of sorry for her, in a way, because, Jesus Christ, what in the world did she do that for? Write all those fantastic lies about my mother. I don't care what she said about me, although it was completely untrue. She had this thing about my mother's funeral where I was supposed to go to a restaurant with her and have this long conversation. Nothing like that ever happened.

She wrote that you were crying.

Well . . . It was just absolutely dotty. It never happened. None of it happened. But mostly it was an incredible lie about my mother. None of the things that she said were true about this *Indian* lover of my mother's. He never existed. The whole thing is absolutely made up.

Didn't her publisher check her story?

Morrow published it. Apparently they didn't consider it necessary to check anything.

They figured you wouldn't sue?

I certainly wouldn't sue. I'm not about to sue anybody about anything. So feel free to do whatever you want to do. (*Laughs.*)

Would your life have been different had you had a brother or sister?

I don't know. I had so many cousins and we all lived together and were all the same age. They were just like brothers and sisters, it really was no difference.

Were you close with them?

Oh, very.

In The Grass Harp, *your character Collin catches a catfish bare-handed. Did you ever do that as a boy?*

Of course.

Is it difficult to do?

Not with a certain kind of experience. I'd catch carp all the time. When I was a child I had a whole stream and it had all kinds of fish. It was like a little river and we built banks which would run in one end and out the other and made a kind of pool. The water had to fall over into it. In the pool I had all *kinds* of fish and I used to reach down and pick them up. They were like kittens to me. I would pet them and put them back in the water.

Is it true that since childhood you haven't been able to recite the alphabet?

No, I can't. I think it's because when I was in the first grade I had a teacher who had a thing against me because I could read so well. I could read since I was four years old. My cousin Sookie taught me, although she could scarcely read herself. I taught her in the end. I can remember reading *Treasure Island* when I was about five. She would get tired and I'd poke her. "Sook, wake up, it's getting interesting here." Reading just seemed like the most natural thing in the world to me.

You could also read upside down, couldn't you?

Mm-hmmm. Anyway, we'd start reciting the alphabet and I'd start to recite it and this teacher would say, "Hold out your palms." And she'd *whack* me across my palms with this ruler and I got a psychosis about it. I couldn't—and cannot—recite it.

If I ask you to try now, would you fault somewhere around P or Q?

I don't know where it would go wrong, but I'll start: A, B, C, D, E, F . . . (*Falters, starts again.*) A, B, C, D, E, F, G, H, I, J . . . Q . . . L, M, N. . . . I don't know.

I believe you. What about math—can you subtract?

I could subtract at one time after I did a lot of things with a tutor, but then, afterwards, it faded away and now I can't subtract. I can add, but I can't subtract.

Were you considered eccentric, even stupid, as a boy?

Actually, I was a very popular child with other kids. I had lots of friends. I think the teachers thought that I was eccentric. What puzzled them was that I was able to read so incredibly well, a thousand times better than anyone else in my classes. Do you remember the WPA during the thirties? They sent these teams of psychiatrists who did I.Q. tests all over the country and there was this whole group that was covering the different parts of the South. They came to the school that I was at at that time in Alabama and I took this I.Q. test. The next day they came back and they asked if I would do the test again, so I did and I scored phenomenally high. I came to New York at their wishes, accompanied by an aunt of mine, to take a special test at the Horace Mann School. That was the first time I came to New York. I was eight years old. And after that I never went back to an ordinary public school. I went to special schools.

Since you began writing around that time, your formative years were really in the South.

Well, after all, everything important really happened to me there. I was sort of on my own, in spite of an incredible number of relatives. I started to write when I was eight years old. I mean, really seriously. So seriously that I dared never mention it to anybody. I spent hours every day writing and never showed it to a teacher.

I used to come home from school and other kids did whatever they did, but I would write for three or four hours every day, just like some kids would practice the piano. It was an obsession.

What were you writing at eight?

Stories. And I also kept a journal. I made a terrible mistake when I was about ten years old. The *Mobile Register* had a contest for readers to submit something that they had written and I took a whole lot of my journal, which was absolutely, literally true, about Mr. and Mrs. Lee, Harper Lee's mother and father, who lived very near. Harper Lee was my best friend. Did you ever read her book, *To Kill a Mockingbird*? I'm a character in that book, which takes place in the same small town in Alabama where we lived. Her father was a lawyer and she and I used to go to trials all the time as children. We went to the trials instead of going to the movies. I was very interested in the law. She actually did go on to law school and became a lawyer. She's living in Alabama practicing law with her sister, Alice Lee, who probably is the most prominent woman lawyer in the South.

Getting back to Mr. and Mrs. Lee.

Mrs. Lee was quite an eccentric character. Mr. Lee was wonderful, but Mrs. Lee—who was a brilliant woman, she could do a *New York Times* crossword puzzle as fast as she could move the pencil, that kind of person—was an endless gossip. So I wrote something called "Mrs. Busybody" about Mrs. Lee and I sent it to the *Mobile Register*. I won second prize and they printed the whole thing and it was just ghastly. It was sort of like when I began publishing those chapters of *Answered Prayers* and everybody was so upset. (*Laughs.*) Well, they were very upset in Alabama.

When you knew it was going to be published, did you have any regrets?

I didn't know it was going to be published! I just sent it in. I never really thought it would be published, much less win a prize. And then one Sunday there it was. Then people started to whisper about me. I'd walk down the street and people on their front porches would pause, fanning for a moment. I found they were very upset about it.

Was that when you became aware of the power of the written word?

I was a little hesitant about showing anything after that. I remember I said, "Oh, I don't know why I did that, I've given up writing." But I was writing more fiercely than ever. (*Laughs.*) While I didn't show anything to anyone, I would submit things. You know the magazine *Scholastic*? I won all of their prizes year after year. One year I won all of them together, short story, everything, and they did a piece about me. I was about eleven years old.

Wasn't that also around the time you ran away with a girl who later grew up to murder a half-dozen people?

Yes. I just knew her one summer. She was living very near me in this little town in Alabama with some relatives of hers. She was sort of a wicked little girl. She was older than I was, at least three years older. She got angry with these people she was staying with and she talked me into running away with her. There was a movie made about her. She was electrocuted at Sing Sing.

Barbra Streisand once told me she wanted to make a movie of the first woman electrocuted in this country.

Oh, I know who she wants to do the movie about. Her name was Ruth something. She'd be great! (*Laughs.*) Ruth—God, they took a photograph of her in the electric chair. I can see why Streisand would like to do it. She really is something, that Streisand. She's always got something up her skirts. I wrote a song that she claims is her favorite song.

Which is?

"A Sleepin' Bee." Which is really the song that started her career. I wrote that song for my play *House of Flowers.* Streisand recorded it on her first record and in her interviews she always says that's her favorite song, but she certainly doesn't do it very well.

Sure she does.

It's good, but it's not as good as Diahann Carroll's, who sang it originally. I don't think much of Diahann Carroll as a singer but she sang it exactly right. Quite a few people have recorded it, but Streisand turned it into a three-act opera and it's not.

She told me once that was a problem for her: even Stevie Wonder once gave her a song but she didn't do it because it didn't have a beginning, middle, and end.

Well, that's Streisand's great fault as a singer, as far as I'm concerned. She takes every ballad and turns it into a three-act opera. She simply cannot leave a song alone.

To return to your writing: weren't you sixteen when you received your first acceptance as a professional writer?

Yes. By the time I was sixteen I was really a competent writer. Technically, I wrote as well then as I do now. Technically. I understood the whole mechanism.

Where did you first publish professionally?

It was the magazine called *Story*, which was a very important literary magazine during the thirties and forties. It was the first magazine to publish Saroyan and, I think, Faulkner. A lot of people. It was a very fine magazine edited by Whit Burnett and Martha Foley and it was the first magazine that I ever sent a story to, which was the one they bought. It was the magazine that I most wanted to have a story published in. The other magazine I wanted to be published in was *The New Yorker.* And within a year of that I'd sent them a story. And shortly after that I went to work at *The New Yorker.*

Not as a writer, though.

No, I was working in the art department. I worked on "Talk of the Town" after a while.

Is there any truth to the story that while you were at The New Yorker, *you appointed yourself an art editor, rejecting submitted drawings you didn't like by dropping them behind the table where you worked?*

No. Where'd you hear that?

It's in Brendan Gill's book.

Well, I was in the art department but I wasn't throwing away people's cartoons.

Didn't Robert Frost get you fired from The New Yorker?

Oh, he was a very mean man. Everybody that ever knew him at all will tell you that. What happened to me was that on my vacation I went to the Breadloaf Writers' Conference—I was only about seventeen. I never liked Robert Frost's poetry and during the course of a conversation he got the idea that I felt rather indifferent toward him. He gave a reading, and while he was reading, a mosquito bit my ankle and I bent to scratch my ankle and sort of slumped over. It looked like I'd fallen asleep, and Robert Frost, who was standing at this podium reading, suddenly slammed his book shut and threw it at me all the way across the room. It missed me but he said, "If that's the way *The New Yorker* feels about my poetry, I won't go on reading," and he stomped out of the room. He then wrote a letter to Harold Ross at *The New Yorker* saying, "How can you send out such a disrespectful person to represent you?" Harold Ross—with whom I was actually quite friendly—wanted an explanation as to what had happened and I said, "Well, I really don't need to give any explanation because I was there on my own, it was my vacation, it had nothing to do with *The New Yorker*." So I left the magazine for about six months, but then I went back.

Well, that accounts for your once calling Frost an "evil, selfish bastard, an egomaniacal, double-crossing sadist."

That's right. (*Laughs.*)

In one of your early stories, "A Tree of Night," that frightening woman says to the college girl, Kay, "What'll you ever learn in a place like that? Let me tell you honey, I'm plenty educated and I never saw the inside of no college." Is that how you feel as well about college, since you never went?

The last thing in the world I would do was waste my time going to college, because I knew what I wanted to do. I had, by that time, read a tremendous amount and was really a very accomplished writer. I had no reason to go to college. The only reason to go to college is if you want to be a doctor, a lawyer, or something in a highly specialized field. But if you want to be a writer, and you *are* a writer already, and you can spell (*laughs*), there's no reason to go to college. Anyway, I went to the best college I could have gone to when I went to work at *The New Yorker*. I couldn't conceivably have gone to a college and learned all that I learned in my two and a half years at *The New Yorker*. It would not have been possible. And besides, I've gotten a lot of degrees.

You began drinking long before you got to The New Yorker, *didn't you? How old were you when you discovered whiskey?*

About twelve. At that time, my mother was married to a very rich man and I was living in this great big mansion in Greenwich, Connecticut. We had a chauffeur who took me to school every day and brought me back and I used to make him go into this liquor store and buy me bottles of blackberry brandy and Old Grand-dad and I'd take it home. Then I would make this perfectly horrible drink which was Old Grand-dad with a jigger of blackberry brandy and I would spend the rest of the afternoon writing and drinking this stuff. At dinnertime I would go downstairs. We had a butler and lots of maids—the whole thing was quite formal—but I would be very merry and laughing at everything. My stepfather said to me once, "I don't know what it is, but you're always so gloomy. You never have anything nice to say about anybody. You're always hiding up in your room, but when you come down to dinner, why, you're as merry as a cricket." (*Laughs.*) That went on for about three years and then it stopped. It didn't stop because of being found out or anything. I just stopped and I don't think I drank again until I was about eighteen.

3

Love, Sex, and Fear

"I'm not promiscuous at all,
I just don't have the energy for it."

Capote's sexuality has never been in question. When he was a boy—according to his mother's sister, Marie Rudisill, who wrote a book about the family which upset Capote—he overheard his mother, Lillie Mae Faulk, telling Little Bit, their black cook, "That boy is so strange, he doesn't look or act like a normal boy. He's just like his father sometimes—little Miss Mouse Fart."

Truman's best friend, his older cousin Sook, used to take him up to the attic and dress him up—"putting a bonnet on his head, slipping faded white arm-length gloves on his hands, wrapping a feathered boa around his neck, and fitting his feet into embroidered slippers...'Pshaw, Tru,' she would say, 'don't you look like an elegant lady ready for the ball!'"

His aunt, whom he called Tiny, wrote about the relationship between Sook and Truman, perhaps the most significant relationship of his childhood. "Sook's love for Truman was almost unnatural in its intensity. In her loneliness she desperately clung to the small boy the way a drowning man clutches his piece of flotsam. Perhaps she sensed in Truman a kindred spirit. They were both forgotten people, Sook by her sisters and brother, Truman by his parents. And both were outsiders—Sook because her childlike innocence kept her apart from the adult world; and Truman because his pretty looks, delicate build, and girlish tendencies offended other people's notions of how a 'real boy' ought to look and act."

(In *Other Voices, Other Rooms,* Capote described how a truck driver, Sam Radclif, eyes the young Joel, "not caring much for the looks of him. He had his notions of what a 'real' boy should look like, and this kid somehow offended them. He was too pretty, too delicate and fair-skinned; each of his features was shaped with a sensitive accuracy, and a girlish tenderness softened his eyes.")

Marie Rudisill recalled the time she and the sixteen-year-old Truman were sitting on the back porch in Monroeville and he said to her, "I will be a brilliant, delicate, sissy, queer, homo—or shall I be formal, darling, and say 'homosexual'?"

In 1976, Capote told Jere Real in the *Advocate*, "When I was at a boarding school at age sixteen, I hadn't been there three weeks and I had already slept with all the boys and about half the faculty! . . . Oh, of course, I'm speaking rhetorically."

In a 1978 interview he gave to *The New York Times Magazine*, Capote said, "I never had any problem with being a homosexual. I mean, look at me. I was always right out there. I was really quite popular. I was amusing and I was pretty. I didn't look like anybody else and I wasn't like anybody else. People start out by being put off by something that's different, but I very easily disarmed them. Seduction—that's what I do. It was: You think I'm different, well, I'll show you how different I really am."

And in *Interview* magazine in 1978, Capote talked about the one lasting relationship of his life. "There is nobody in the world that you can't get if you really concentrate on it, if you really want them. You've got to want it to the exclusion of everything else. That's how I got novelist Jack Dunphy. Everybody said I could never get him, he was married to a terrific girl, Joan McCracken. I liked her too, very much. I was just determined. I concentrated on it to the exclusion of everything else. It turned out it was a good thing on all fronts.... Whatever relationship you have, man or woman, you have to be very attentive and you have to be a very good friend to them.... If you can't be friends with a lover, then forget it. It's not going to work."

You've said that you feel E. M. Forster is the finest English novelist of this century.

I think he's one of them.

Did he once complain to you that all of his life he was a prisoner of his sexual imagination?

Mm-hmmm.

Is that true for you as well?

I don't know. He said to me that when he was a young man all he thought about was sex. He was obsessed by sex and he kept thinking, "How wonderful it will be when I'm forty and I'll have eased up on all of this." And when he was forty it got worse. He thought, "My gosh, when I get to be fifty I'll have some relief." At fifty it was worse and he said, "Surely, by the time I'm sixty..." Then suddenly he was seventy and seventy-five and he said, "I'm seventy-five years old and it's worse than it ever was. I'm finding myself thinking about it continuously now that I can hardly do anything about it." I've told that to a number of people and they all agreed that they felt that way about themselves. I'm talking about older people. I've never been that way so I can't really answer for myself. I've never been a person with a wandering, whimsical imagination.

In your lifetime, Truman, how promiscuous have you been?

Not very.

In that piece "Nocturnal Turnings," your "Siamese twin" complains to you that he'd much prefer solitary satisfaction to some of the duds you've forced him to endure. How many duds have there been?

Well, I don't know. In everybody's life there's quite a plethora, isn't there?

He—that is, your other self—said he would have preferred being spared the misery of many of your encounters. How miserable have some of your relationships been?

Actually, if truth be known, I'd say only about three.

In your "Self-Portrait" in The Dogs Bark, *you wrote about standing at a window on a Mediterranean island watching a boat arrive with someone who had said good-bye to you and had apparently changed his mind. You asked yourself, "Is it the real turtle soup?—or only the mock? Or is it at long last love? (It was.)" Do you remember that?*

I know what you're talking about but it's all rather vague in my memory now. But what about it? It was somebody I had a quarrel with and he left and then he came back on the next boat, right? So what? Big deal. That happens all the time. I have arguments with people in restaurants, they walk out, they come back before dessert's served. (*Laughs.*)

What is it that attracts you to someone? Is it more physical or intellectual?

It has to be pretty much both. But anyway, I'm never attracted to quite anybody anymore.

You've been with Jack Dunphy for twenty-five years now, haven't you?

Thirty-five.

Do you have an understanding about seeing other people?

I told you, I don't have nothing to do with anybody

at all anymore. Before Jack, I had one relationship and two walkouts. And that's it. I'm not promiscuous at all, I just don't have the energy for it and I don't care about it. If I get involved with somebody I get involved too much, you know. It's not just like I go to bed with someone. First of all, I don't find that many people attractive. That's more my fault than theirs. That's quite a lot, really: to have had four fairly large affairs and one full-time, lifelong one.

What kind of person is Jack?

He's a fabulous person. He lives in the other house—the homey homier house [in Sagaponack]. He's a great skier and he's written six or seven really marvelous books. His last book, *First Wine*, got very good press. And he's just finishing a book called *Yesterday's Dancers.*

Would you consider writing an introduction to his latest book?

In this particular book it would be ridiculous for anybody except George Balanchine to write an introduction to it. It's a marvelous, terrific book.

Do the two of you eat out often?

I don't eat out at night ever. Jack loves to cook. We have this table by the fireplace and we eat there. I never accept an invitation. I always say I just left yesterday for New York.

Are you a jealous person?

Yes. Not about friends, but if I have a certain emotional attachment to somebody, I'm likely to be jealous. I get over it fairly soon, but I go through a period of being jealous.

Is it an emotion you dislike in yourself or is it something you've accepted?

No, I don't like it.

How long do those periods last?

Not too long. When I feel it, I usually begin to counteract it—a certain distance grows between me and the person. It's my doing. It's not good. It's always bad for me if I start feeling any kind of jealousy about somebody.

You've written that few of us know that love is tenderness, few people understand that. What do you think most people think love is?

Sex.

Seriously?

Mm-hmmm.

You don't think most people separate the two?

I think it has to sort of begin in their heads as sex and then it can change into something else. If you're just talking about between individuals, not between parents and children and things like that. That's a different kind of love. This man Gerald Clarke who's writing this book about me—do you know him? He's one of the lead writers at *Time* magazine. He's really a very good writer. His book, it better be fantastic, because he's worked on it for eight years. I've never known such research. This is the first book he's ever written. I don't want to read it, but he certainly knows more about me than anybody else does, including myself. He's interviewed people I went to school with when I was five years old. If you can tell the truth, it's a very interesting story. Not a lot of nonsense like that stupid book by my aunt. Anyway, he told me the other day about someone I had known very well when I was seventeen, eighteen years old, this girl that I liked a lot and who was a great friend of mine. He had interviewed this girl and she had told him that I had asked her to marry me many times, and all I could think was: *What*? (*Laughs.*) I thought, well, Gerald, you researchers do come up with some fantastic information. And I'm not talking about Harper Lee. That's been the story of her life—that I spent my childhood asking her to marry me. I spent my childhood asking her to keep her hands out of my pants. (*Long laugh.*) There's more truth than fiction in that.

There once was something in print about your once having asked someone to marry you early in your life.

It's news to me.

Have you ever felt that you would like to have been a father or raised a child?

No. I mean, I don't dislike children. I like children very much. I have a lot of friends who have children. I like animals, though. I've always been very good with animals and I've always had a lot of them.

Have you ever killed an animal?

I killed two things in my life, both of them birds, and I regretted it bitterly. I don't have the heart for it. I have the eye, but I don't have the heart. I'm a very good shot, actually. I haven't shot in seven years, but I'm a very good pistol shot. I can do a wonderful trick. I'm sure I could do it tomorrow morning. I have these tin cans thrown up in the air and a thirty-eight-caliber revolver and I can shoot all of them out of the air as fast as they go up.

Do you own a gun now?

I don't have one. I had a thirty-eight-caliber revolver, a very, very good gun, but it was stolen.

Is shooting something you never forget how to do?

It's something you always know, like riding a bike. I began when I was about eight years old and then I did it in school a great deal.

(We were sitting at a table at Bobby Van's in Bridgehampton at this point of our conversation. Truman was drinking doubles

of his "usual" and after a few hours I asked him if he wanted anything to eat. "Sure I do," he said, "but once you order something to eat, it comes so fast—shebang!—you never get to finish your drink."

When we finally ordered, Truman wanted shrimp with tartar sauce but they were out of the sauce so he settled for a grilled-cheese-bacon-and-tomato sandwich with a bowl of chili. "Jack would highly disapprove of this," he said. "Anything fried. Jack only believes in fish and chicken, fresh vegetables and fruit. I don't like peanut butter and jelly," he continued, "but I like a really good egg-salad sandwich or a really good chicken-salad sandwich."

Before we ordered, however, Truman decided to have a little fun with the waitress, Barbara—a woman who seemed to know him well and who obviously cared for him. "What little children are you going to chop up today?" he chided.

"Now, be good, Truman, or this gentleman won't come back."

"That's why he's here," Truman said. "He's heard about the wonderful cannibal dish that you put cantaloupe in. In fact, they're bringing out a book called Bobby Van's Cannibal Cookbook*."*

"We'll take a few of the leftover summer people and make a dish out of them," Barbara said.

"Especially the ones who leave their dogs," Truman added. "There are two people that are hateful: the ones who walk off without paying their bills and the ones who bring animals out here for the summer and drive away and leave them. I could just kill them. I'm on the staff of ARF—the Animal Rescue Foundation. We go around collecting these animals. It's so terrible, it's ghastly. Don't you think that's vile? These people come out to the country with these animals to amuse their children and then when it's time to go back they don't want them, so they tie them to the doorknob and drive away. We do a lot of rescuing, because if they're not

rescued they have to be put away. I've got people to take more dogs and cats—their houses are full of them now. The minute they see me they go, 'Arf arf. . . . bleech!'")

Were your own pets mostly dogs?

I've lived in several places and used to cart four or five dogs and cats, but it was too much. I have a house in Switzerland—funny, all animals love Switzerland. You could just let them out the door, it's so safe up there in the mountains, they just run around, know when to come home, you don't have to worry about them. You can do that here, too.

Maybe that's what these summer tourists are doing—figuring if they leave their pets here, they'll eventually find their way back over the ninety miles to Manhattan.

(*Laughs.*) My last dog died two years ago. I had her sixteen years and I loved her so much. I just couldn't get over when she died. I can't go through this again, soon. You get so attached to them, it's terrible. Terrible when they die. It's so painful.

Did you have to put her away?

I had to. She was perfectly healthy in every way except that her back two legs were paralyzed and she couldn't walk. I went through a year of that, carrying her to peepee, to do everything. And she wasn't unhappy, that was the most terrible part. And she wasn't unhealthy, either. But there was a point where there was nothing more I could do. I had a friend take her. But the friend was a good friend of hers. It would have been too horrible for me. I'd done it once before with another dog—it made me so ill, I was in bed for three weeks.

Dogs have figured in two personal incidents in your life and one macabre but humorous story, about a friend of yours you set up on a date with a woman who lived at the Dakota and had a Great Dane....

I didn't set him up to meet her. This guy had a crush on this girl, a very well-known model. He arranged to take her to dinner and the theater. When he arrived at her apartment in the Dakota the maid answered the door and said the young lady was getting dressed, would he go into the living room and make himself a drink. So he went into this big room that had French windows which were open. He saw this enormous Great Dane lying on the floor, playing with a ball. It was obvious that the dog wanted him to play with him. So he goes over, picks up the ball, and bounces it against this big plain white wall. The dog jumps up and grabs it, runs back and hands it to him. He throws it against the wall again and this goes on for about five minutes. Suddenly he throws the ball and it glanced against the wall and went out the window. The dog took one look and followed it right out the window! There was this horrible crash. At just this moment, the girl came into the room saying, "Oh, I'm so terribly sorry, we're going to be late for the theater." He was just speechless with horror and didn't know what to do or say. She kept saying, "Hurry, hurry, hurry—the elevators in this building are slow." So they went to the theater and he didn't say a word. She became more and more mystified. Here was this guy who was supposed to have a fabulous crush on her and he wouldn't even speak to her. During the intermission she said, "I don't understand what's the matter with you, but you're making me frightfully nervous and I'm going home." Then she said, "I forgot to feed my dog. Did you see my dog?" "Yes," he said, "I did. And I must say he looked awful hungry and despondent." She walked out, went home, and the dog was in the courtyard. Along with John Lennon.

Didn't you have a frightening experience with some Dobermans when you visited Doris Duke in Hawaii?

I was staying in her house and she had all these Doberman pinschers that patrolled the grounds, but I didn't know that because I had just arrived. And I walked out the door and suddenly about sixteen Doberman pinschers surrounded me and they kind of held me. For about three hours I couldn't move, because if I did, they'd attack me. Finally a gardener came along and all he did was blow a whistle and they scattered. But I'll always remember it. It was very frightening. It's very difficult to stand completely still for three hours.

Did you think of anything during that time or did you blank out your mind?

All I could think of was standing still. (*Laughs.*)

It was a dog that almost got you killed in a car accident in 1966, wasn't it?

Mm-hmmm. I was on a lonely country road and I was driving in a convertible and I had a little four-month-old puppy in the car, sitting beside me. She jumped up and jumped in the back and was sliding out of the car. I reached around to try to grab her and I lost control of the car and there was only one tree on that whole road and the car ran into it headfirst. And I went through the windshield. I had to have a lot of plastic work done on my face. I had terrible cuts and scars and whatnot. But I was very fortunate because the first car that came along was a nurse and her husband. I kept losing consciousness and coming to and she managed to stop the bleeding partially and they ran to a house and got an ambulance that took me to the hospital.

Do you remember what you were thinking about while you were lying there in semiconsciousness?

I kept reciting the telephone numbers of everybody I could remember.

As a way of staying conscious?

Yeah, mm-hmmm.

You must have had a lot of numbers in your head. How many friends, Truman, do you trust completely?

About seven or eight.

Are they friends of a lifetime?

They're friends of a long time. Most of my lifetime friends, like Cecil B. De Mille, are gone. Noël, Cecil . . . all the friends I count when I was sixteen years old, most of them are gone.

Do you meet new people now and befriend them? Or is there too much to do in your life to make new friends?

There really is too much to do, and I have enough friends as it is. Friendship is a pretty full-time occupation if you really are friendly with somebody. You can't have too many friends because then you're just not really friends. Friends that I count are friends that if they went to the hospital, I'd go every day to see them. You just can't have too much of that going on, especially with the people I know who are always going to be in some kind of . . . well, actually, most of the friends I have are really very strong, very secure people.

Wasn't Adlai Stevenson a friend of yours?

Adlai was a very good friend of mine. A *very* good friend. I knew him long before he first ran for President. I was with him the very day he died. In fact, I spent the night with him the night before he died. In the *same* bedroom. (*Slightly wicked laugh.*)

How did that come about?

We were living together in the ambassador's house in London. (*Laughs.*) This is a fact.

Was it a loving relationship?

I won't go beyond saying we were *very good* friends.

If you were living together, one would have to assume you were.

Well, not necessarily. There was a shortage of space. (*Laughs.*)

Was he a sick man?

No, he was in very good health. We had a lot to drink the night before and were laughing. And the next morning he left to go out to meet Marietta Tree to go for an appointment somewhere and he dropped dead on the sidewalk.

How shocked were you?

I was amazed. I was still in the room when they came in to pack his clothes. I'm telling you the truth. Suddenly this army of people were in the bedroom taking all of his clothes out of it and I heard that he had died. I was absolutely stunned because he was going to leave with me the next day to go on a cruise in Greece. So you can see we were very good friends.

Have you ever written about Stevenson?

No, but he appears in *Answered Prayers* toward the end.

As himself?

As himself.

How different might things have been had he been elected and not Eisenhower?

Well... I don't know what I would have done to the Rose Garden! (*Laughs.*)

A number of your friends over the years have been women. You've written that a woman doesn't deserve full marks until she attains and maintains qualities of style and appearance and amus-

ing good sense beyond the point of easy youthful beguilement.

I believe that.

Who are the women whom you give full marks to today?

They're all dead. Barbara Paley was the person I was thinking of when I said that. She had everything.

Did you also have Lee Radziwill in mind as well?

No, not Lee. I never thought of Lee as anything except a rather spoiled child. And I felt rather sorry for her.

What about Oona Chaplin?

Yes, Oona's like that. She's a good person—a mature, fine person. Morella Agnelli has that quality. You know, Nancy Reagan's not a bad one. She really isn't. She doesn't have the stature of a person like Barbara Paley with the strength of real character, but she's got something going for her that's not bad at all. She's a little fragile and frail compared to these women I'm talking about, but she has character, strength about her. I admire Nancy. I admired Mrs. Nixon. I think she is an extraordinary woman to have survived all that she has and with the dignity she has. Don't you? I've known every First Lady since Mrs. Roosevelt with the exception of Mrs. Nixon, but I admire her because she's shown enormous discretion in her life and I feel very sorry for her. She's really suffered, and so unnecessarily, and she's been very dignified about it. She's a woman of interesting mystery. She's one of the few women that I know if a magazine asked me to do a portrait of somebody—which they're always asking me to do—she's one of the few people that I would do, because I think she's fascinating and I would like to know more about her than I do know... or anybody knows.

What other women do you admire?

Queen Elizabeth is a woman of character. Garbo is, if you know her. She's a woman of her own beliefs who's lived up to them, never swerved. I think she's very intelligent. Elizabeth Taylor is a person that I admire, she has character. She stands up for what she thinks and believes and lives a life, hard as it is, one way or the other. Mrs. King, Coretta King, had a hard road to hoe, certainly a very admirable woman.

How about Mother Teresa? What do you think of her?

Well . . . I'm always dubious about saints, aren't you? (*Laughs.*) I find them *all* suspicious. I think the present pope is an excellent woman in drag. And I kid you not!

Would you like to write a profile on him?

Write a profile on the pope? I think he's a real phony, so I don't think I'd be interested in him at all—because I know it would turn out to be completely negative.

Phony in what ways?

Oh, *I* bothered to read his novel! (*Laughs.*) After that, mon cher, ask no more!

Getting back to women, in your story "Mojave," you wrote that "Women are like flies: they settle on sugar or shit." Is there nothing in between?

I didn't say that, a character says it. You can't blame a writer for what the characters say.

Well, how do you feel about that statement?

It's pretty harsh and hard, but I believe that that particular character would definitely believe it and he had every reason to.

Those kinds of remarks offend a lot of feminists. Does that bother you at all? Have the advances they've made affected you as a writer?

I don't know what advances they've made. I've never understood it. I'm a big newspaper reader, I read at least three or four and about ten magazines a week, so I'd say I was pretty well informed, but I don't know what advances women think they have made or what it is that they thought they were up against.

Equal pay for one. Women earn fifty-nine cents to every dollar a man makes for the same work.

There's probably a good reason for that.

What?

A man works harder.

You really believe that?

Yes.

That should raise some eyebrows, Truman.

Well, I think the men *do* work harder.

In every field? Lawyers, doctors . . . ?

Boy, never send me to another woman doctor. I had a woman doctor who should have been put in a cage and sent to Hong Kong to be sold in the slave market.

Recently?

Four years ago. She was unbelievable. I had to have an injection which had to be in my hip. She wouldn't give it to me there, she gave it in my arm and I was suddenly paralyzed for two and a half weeks. I told her at the very moment she was doing it that you cannot give me this injection in my arm and she said, "Nonsense," and wham!

Does that mean all *women doctors are taboo for you?*

I wouldn't have nothing to do with any of them. Occasionally you have nurses who are good.

Are you going back to the position that a woman's place is in her home?

No, they can do what they want to do but just keep quiet about it. (*Laughs.*) There's no sense making all this fuss all the time.

What about the Equal Rights Amendment? Should there be one?

That's all just been fakery and hooey. And poor Ronald Reagan's being dragged through the streets by horses—what do these old broads want, anyway? They're lucky to be allowed to have a roof over their heads. It's very interesting about women, anyway. There've been some great women writers, but have there been any great women in any other thing?

How about artists? Georgia O'Keeffe, for instance.

Hack, hack, hack. I wouldn't pay twenty-five cents to spit on a Georgia O'Keeffe painting. And I think she's a horrible person, too. I know her.

Why is she so horrible?

So arrogant, so sure of herself. I'm sure she's carrying a dildo in her purse.

Let's go on to the issue of abortion. Do women have a right to abortion?

Yes. Of course women have a right to have an abortion. I don't understand why anybody doesn't have a right to things on that level.

Back to "Mojave" for another comment. This time, a character says, "There's two things I'm scared of. Snakes and women. They have a lot in common. One thing they have in common is: the last thing that dies is their tail."

That's something an old uncle of mine used to say. I just gave it to the character. This old Uncle Bud would always say, "A woman's just like a snake, the last thing that dies is her tail."

And you never asked what that meant?

I knew what it meant.

Are you, yourself, scared of women... and snakes?

No. I always am very friendly with women. I was bitten by a cottonmouth moccasin when I was nine years old, in the toe. I spent a very rocky three months, but I'm not afraid of snakes.

Didn't you once kill a rattlesnake with a garden hoe?

No, that was my cousin Sookie, from "A Christmas Memory." I have a thing about snakes. You haven't seen my apartment, but I have a fabulous collection of all kinds of snakes that decorate a whole room. It's a room that frightens some people but it's really very pretty. I do these collages of boxes and a lot of the themes have to do with serpents.

Sounds Freudian.

In my case, I don't think so.

A lot of writers seem to like to dabble in the visual arts. Do you paint as well?

I don't paint but I do these collages. I take boxes and then I cover them with different kinds of paper and then I do collages on top of the boxes. Then I fill them with sort of secret surprises. You can open them up and find some fairly amazing things inside. They're highly unusual, very curious. I'm supposedly going to have a show of them at the Gotham Gallery. The boxes are all being set inside of a big framework made of plaster so that you can see all sides. It has mirrors and light—terrific lighting effects. So you can see all the boxes from every conceivable angle. They're rather flashy and very colorful.

Do you do them for friends or just for yourself?

I do it for myself. I find it very relaxing.

How superstitious are you?

Very. Just about as superstitious as anybody you've ever met.

You won't step on a crack, walk under a ladder, cross a black cat's path . . . ?

Just begin with A, end with Z, and forget it! (*Laughs.*)

What's wrong with yellow roses?

(*Gasps.*) Oh, let's just don't go into that. Don't bring it up! Don't *start.*

What about three cigarette butts in an ashtray?

Oh, well, that's terrible. Since I don't smoke anymore, it doesn't bother me.

But that's unlucky?

Oh, very.

What about the day Friday?

It's not a preferable day. I got a bit over it just being Friday, but it's not one of the better days.

What's the best day?

Wednesday is the best day. Tuesdays, Wednesdays, and Thursdays are all all right. The rest are very debatable. (*Laughs.*)

If you're on a plane and there are two nuns on it...

Oh, forget it.

You won't fly?

I'll get off. I'll get out of the seat, anyway.

Does it have to be two?

Just two. One by herself doesn't matter. You'll just have a crash and everybody will be killed except you. (*Laughs.*)

Why are nuns unlucky?

Oh, they just are. They're a bunch of monsters. (*Laughs.*)

We've talked of women and snakes, which don't scare you. What does?

I'm not afraid of the things that most people are afraid of. I'm not afraid of murderers. I know too many of them. I'm not afraid of crime in the sense that most people seem to be afraid of it. In fact, I had a very amusing experience about four years ago on First Avenue. I was walking home about two o'clock in the morning in the Fifties on First Avenue and suddenly these three fellows, sort of Hispanic types, were coming along the sidewalk right in front of me. And I knew by the way that they spread out that they were going to rob me or mug me or do something. I had a fountain pen in my pocket and I pulled it out as they were coming and I said, "Ladies and gentlemen, this is Station WNEW. You're about to witness a mugging right on First Avenue. This is Truman Capote speaking." I went on talking and they started to laugh and they walked me home.

That still doesn't answer the question. What are you scared of?

Well, I don't like being alone over too long a period of time. Like all those months I was alone in Switzerland in this remote place working on *In Cold Blood*, or all those months and years that I was in and out of Kansas, living alone in these strange motels and whatnot. I found it rather frightening. Something about it was unsettling.

The writer's life. Do you think writers become writers because there's nothing else they could have done about it? Or is that too romantic a notion?

If I could have been anything other than a writer, I would have liked to have been a lawyer. I think I would have made a marvelous lawyer. I don't know how happy I would have been.

Do you feel you've had a happy life as a writer?

Partially.

How much has luck played in your career?

None. Nothing lucky ever happened to me.

4

Writing

"It's a very excruciating life
facing that blank piece of paper
every day and having to reach up
somewhere into the clouds and bring
something down out of them."

Capote had been writing stories for years, was even recognized for them in the early 1940's by *Scholastic* magazine; and then, at nineteen, he won the first of three O. Henry awards for his short story "Miriam," a strange, macabre tale of a young girl who enters the mind and life of a middle-aged woman and destroys her. He attempted a novel, which he called *Summer Crossing*, but it seemed "thin, clever, unfelt"—and he threw it away.

"Another language, a secret spiritual geography, was burgeoning inside me, taking hold of my nightdream hours as well as my wakeful daydreams," he wrote in 1969.

That language, that geography, came to him on a frosty December afternoon during a walk in a forest, "along the bank of a mysterious, deep, very clear creek." As the story took shape, he got lost in those woods, "for my mind was reeling with the whole book."

When he finally reached home, he went straight to his room, locked the door, got into bed fully clothed, "and with pathetic optimism, wrote: '*Other Voices, Other Rooms*—a novel by Truman Capote.' Then: 'Now a traveller must make his way to Noon City by the best means he can...'"

It was a sensational debut for Capote. The New York *Herald Tribune* called it "the most exciting first novel by a young American in many years."

There were images and sentences which dazzled: a "wagon's rickety wheels made dust clouds that hung in the green air like powdered bronze." A black man's face "was like a black withered apple, and almost destroyed; his polished forehead shone as though a purple light gleamed under the skin; his sickle-curved posture made him look as though his back were broken: a sad little brokeback dwarf crippled with age."

His contemporary William Styron was impressed that this young writer had arrived full-blown on the literary scene, calling him "an extremely gifted writer, a man of almost unique talents."

"He was a full-fledged master of the language before he was old enough to vote," Styron said. "I was nearly sick with envy. He could make words dance and sing, change colors mysteriously, perform feats of magic, provoke laughter, send a chill up the back, touch the heart."

His high-school English teacher, Catherine Wood, proudly said, "I always recognized Truman's genius and felt we should make allowances for it. Writing was the only subject he was interested in. Other subjects simply did not exist."

Critic Diana Trilling wrote in *The Nation* that he had "the ability to bend language to his poetic moods."

Somerset Maugham called him "the hope of modern literature."

There was little doubt that a major talent had thrown his hat into the literary ring. And though he would not publish as prolifically as some of his peers, when his work did appear it *was* noticed, often optioned for the movies, and very widely read. A book of stories (*A Tree of Night*, 1949) and another of travel pieces (*Local Color*, 1950) preceded his second novel, *The Grass Harp* (1951). His next book was a journalistic tour de force called *The Muses Are Heard*, satiric reportage about a Russian tour by an all-black American *Porgy and Bess* company. His now-classic novella *Breakfast at Tiffany's* appeared two years later.

Capote's ability to accurately hear and report was dramatically illustrated when *In Cold Blood* appeared in 1965. *Life* hailed it as a "masterpiece." The *New York Review of Books* called it "the best documentary account of an American crime ever written." *The New York Times* said it was "remarkable, tensely exciting, moving, superbly written."

Other journalistic pieces followed, collected in *The Dogs Bark* and *Music for Chameleons*. And then came the chapters from *Answered Prayers*, published in four installments in *Esquire* in the mid-seventies. The title came from a quote from Saint Thérèse, who said: "More tears are shed over answered prayers than unanswered ones." Every word he published seemed to create a stir.

"I've known all my life I could take a bunch of words and throw them up in the air and they would come down just right," he asserted. "I'm a semantic Paganini."

In your preface to Music for Chameleons, *you wrote that "When God hands you a gift, he also hands you a whip; and the whip is intended solely for self-flagellation." What did you mean by that?*

By that I meant that God does give one a gift, whatever it may be, composing or writing, but for whatever pleasure it may bring, it also is a very painful thing to live with. It's a very excruciating life, facing that blank piece of paper every day and having to reach up somewhere into the clouds and bring something down out of them. I mean, I'm always quite, quite nervous at the beginning of my workday. It takes me a great deal of time to get started. Once I get started, it gradually calms down a bit, but I'll do anything to keep postponing. I must have five hundred pencils sharpened that I'll resharpen down to nothing. Anyway, one way or another, I manage to write about four hours a day.

Where do you usually like to write?

Actually, I do a lot of writing in bed.

How productive do you feel you are?

I don't know what you mean by that.

If writing is such a struggle for you...

Not the actual writing. The struggle is before, getting

myself on the launching pad. (*Laughs.*) I hate getting onto the launching pad. Once I'm launched, I'm all right.

When you finish writing for the day, do you leave off in the middle of a paragraph or with your first sentence of the next paragraph to get you back into the next day's work?

Yes, I always have done that trick. It's a good trick.

But it's still a nerve-racking experience?

Mm-hmmm.

How much of your work do you reread before you start writing new words?

What I do is, I work four hours a day and then usually early in the evening I read over what I've written during the day and I do a lot of changing and shifting around. See, I write in longhand and I do two versions of whatever I'm doing. I write first on yellow paper and then I write on white paper and then when I finally have it more or less settled the way I want, then I type it. When I'm typing it, that's when I do my final rewrite. I almost never change a word after that.

Have you ever used a secretary?

P. O'Shea is a lady who was my secretary...

Isn't that the name you're listed under in the directory for Sagaponack?

Yes, I always thought I should have *some* number listed. (*Laughs.*) She's a good friend. All my secretaries have been good friends, but I just can't stand secretaries. I can't stand having them around because I have this horrible feeling that they're sitting and waiting for me to deliver something for them to do. It's a perpetual sense of guilt. I feel as though I'm back in grammer school.

Rod Serling used to sit by his pool and talk his stories into a tape recorder, and then have them transcribed.

I think it's impossible, in a literary sense, to dictate

your work. Henry James had to, the last third of his life, and it just amazes me that you can tell instantly whether a page was dictated or whether it was written. Because the dictated ones are always infinitely more elaborate. I think it's quite amazing that he dictated *The Turn of the Screw.*

Steve Allen told me he talks everything he does—books, scripts, songs, ideas—into a Dictaphone and has a pool of secretaries ready to transcribe his every word.

And it's all shit! So it must be the toilet pool. I despise him. I think he's so insensitive. I've a couple of times been on television programs like with Johnny Carson or Merv Griffin, but with him, you sometimes pop your ears because you can't believe what he just said. As for talent, I wouldn't even know whether he's talented or not, there's nothing that he's ever done that interests me. I wouldn't read his books or watch his TV programs. (*Pauses.*) Do you keep a journal?

Yes. You do, too, don't you?

Mm-hmmm. It's very useful.

Do you make daily entries?

No, I don't keep it daily but I maybe do it twice a week. In the two days I do it, I catch up on what happened in the past.

Are you writing it for posterity or as notes for future use? Do you use dialogue or enter notes and fragments?

I do dialogue and description. In my journal I have my special list of truly despicable people. It's run now to something over four thousand names.

Who are some of the people you have high up on that list?

Oh gosh! Come back to that while my mind races around thinking about it.

You started doing a column of observations for Esquire *recently. Is that where your journal comes in handy?*

LIFE
'In Cold Blood' is filmed on scene of the crime
NIGHTMARE REVISITED
In Kansas, Truman Capote stands between actors who play killers in movie of his book
MAY 12 · 1967 · 35¢

Scott Wilson, Capote, and Robert Blake in Kansas for the filming of *In Cold Blood.* Said Robert Blake: "Capote taught me more about acting than anyone."

Of Monroe, Capote wrote: "Marilyn! Marilyn, why did everything have to turn out the way it did? Why does life have to be so fucking rotten?"

With Norman Mailer, 1978. After Norman Mailer published *The Executioner's Song*, Capote said: "I spent six years on *In Cold Blood*, but Mailer never even met Gary Gilmore. He was just a rewrite man like you have over at the *Daily News*."

Capote appeared drunk on stage at Towson State University in Maryland in November, 1977. "Something happened that threw me into an absolute fury and I walked off, saying terrible things in front of 5,000 people."

With Lee Radziwill, 1969. Capote blamed Princess Lee Radziwill and her sister, Jacqueline Onassis, for their silence when Gore Vidal sued him for libel. It was the end of a once beautiful friendship with both sisters.

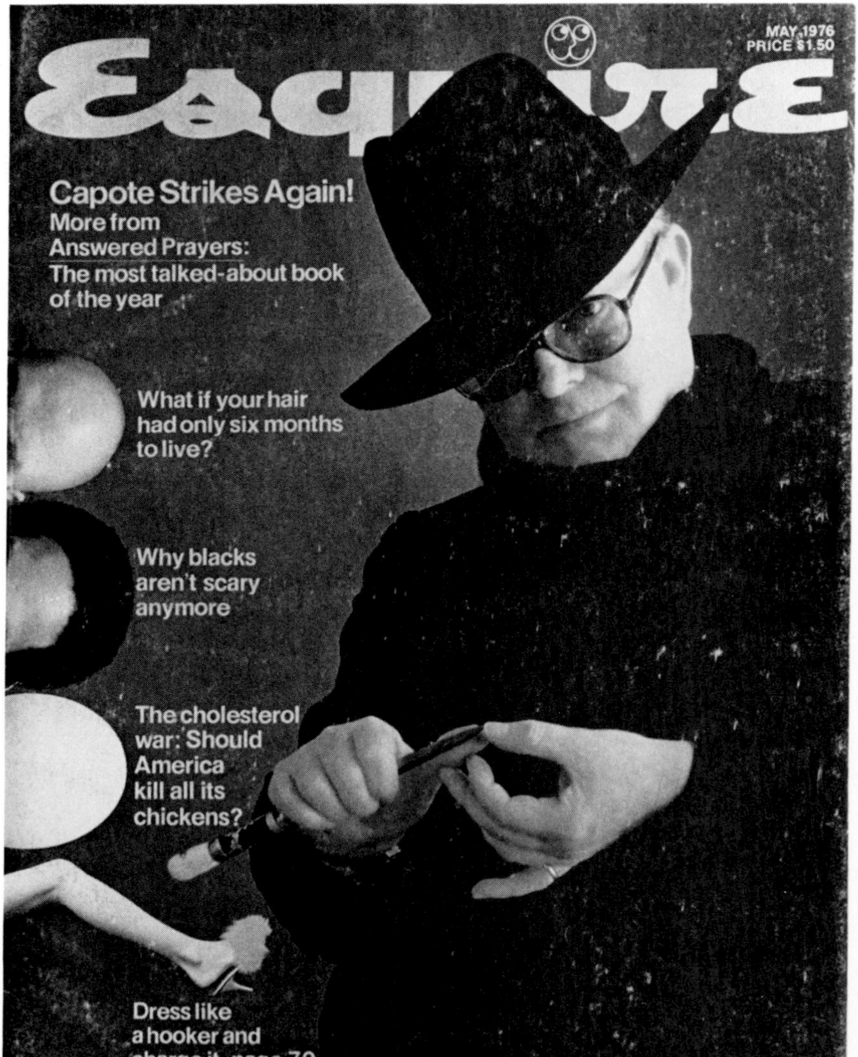

The chapters from *Answered Prayers* created a storm of controversy, and Capote found himself suddenly shunned by those he felt he knew—and understood—so well. He came to believe it was a mistake publishing anything.

With Andy Warhol. "When he was a child, Andy Warhol had this obsession about me. When he came to New York, he used to stand outside my house just waiting for me to come out. He nearly drove me crazy."

With James Jones (left), Willie Morris (second from right), and John Knowles. Capote often ate at Bobby Van's in Bridgehampton, where Lawrence Grobel recorded two of their conversations. Capote's favorite drink was a double Stolichnaya with two blocks of ice and grapefruit juice on the side.

© UPI/Bettmann Archive

Capote was a frequent habitué of Studio 54. "We smoked Thai sticks and danced for hours."

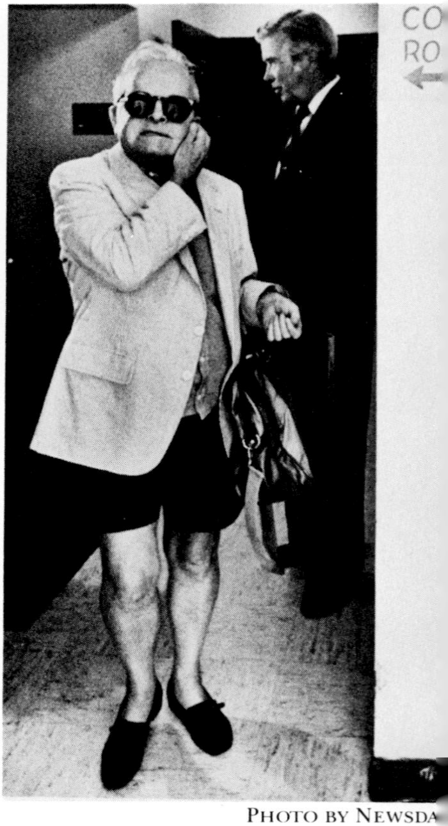

In the summer of 1983, Capote was arrested for drunken driving without a license, and he outraged the judge by appearing in court wearing shorts. "He was very insulted that I was taking the whole thing so casually. Actually, I looked quite smart. I had a very smart pair of shorts on and a very smart jacket and shirt and sandals."

Photo by Newsda

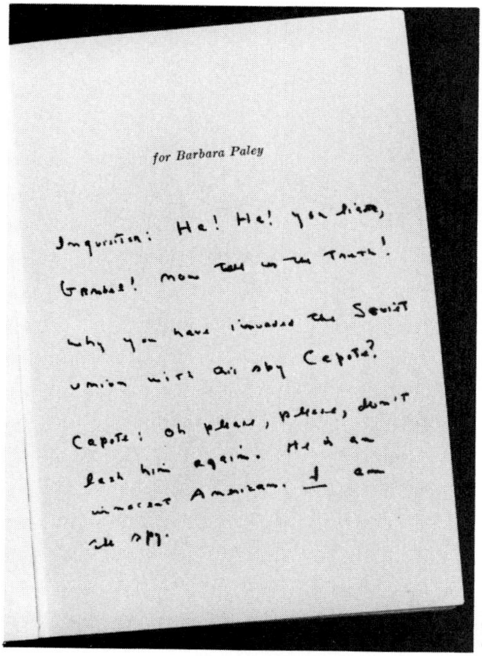

Capote wrote in Lawrence Grobel's copy of *The Muses Are Heard:* "*Inquisitor:* He! He! You liar, Grobel! Now tell us the truth! Why you have invaded the Soviet Union with air spy Capote? *Capote:* Oh please, please, don't lash him again. He is an innocent American. *I* am the spy." Then he read it over and laughed, "Hmmm, this is pretty good, maybe I should publish it."

© LARRY LOGAN

With Lawrence Grobel.

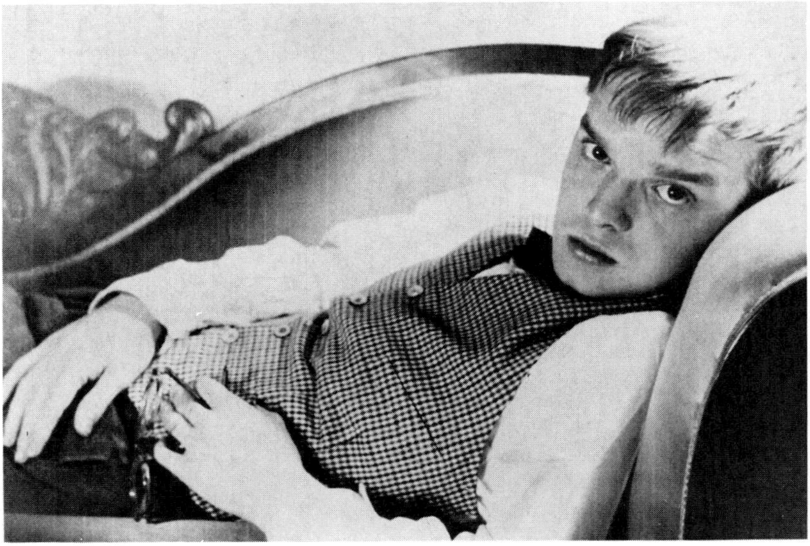

© HALMA

The picture that appeared on the back of *Other Voices, Other Rooms,* and helped launch a career. "I didn't see anything wrong with it," Capote said. "It's just me lying on the sofa looking at the camera. But I guess it assumes that I'm more or less beckoning somebody to climb on top of me."

© HARVEY WANG

Truman liked this portrait by Harvey Wang. "It's the kind of picture you send to an old lover and say, 'It's a good thing you left or look what you would have ended up with.' "

Why do you think I wrote it? I always knew one day it would come in useful. The one I'm doing now is on Cole Porter. Cole was one of my greatest friends, but I tell about naughty things. (*Laughs.*) I don't leave myself out of it, but I don't leave Cole out of it! If people were amazed at my gall in *Answered Prayers*, they're going to have a special session of Congress to see that my passport is never renewed.... (*Laughs.*)

Weren't you originally supposed to write a column for the new Vanity Fair?

Haven't you been following the press coverage about all that? Everyone in New York is really interested in it, it's on TV all the time. It's all favorable to me, which is quite amazing to me. Well, *Vanity Fair* is full of a bunch of bums. Thus it goes. I don't say nothing, they don't say nothing, but the newspapers manage to fill whole pages about my leaving them and going to *Esquire*. Maybe *Esquire* is doing it. (*Laughs.*)

What happened?

I had a big falling-out with *Vanity Fair*. Well, listen ...this man who is the editor (*laughs*)—Sy Newhouse owns it—well, you know. (*Laughs.*) They put this idiot man from *The New York Times Book Review*... When I saw the layout, it's like Radio City, 1935. Art deco in all the wrong ways. So I withdrew from it. I took the piece I wrote back. I'm doing it for *Esquire* just to undo *Vanity Fair* and I'm *really* going to undo them! The first one is so good it makes anything at *Vanity Fair* seem like a little Southern boy with a worm on a hook trying to catch a shark. It appeared on the exact same day as *Vanity Fair* came out. (*Delighted laugh.*) *Vanity Fair*'s the flop of the century! Almost the entire staff was fired. Sy Newhouse was in such a rage, he sent a memo down that he wanted everybody's desk cleaned out in two days and he didn't want to see any of those faces in the building again. It got the worst reviews of anything since the revival of *Private Lives.*

You get between fifteen and twenty thousand dollars for your magazine pieces. Does your fiction suffer because of the time you put into journalism?

No, not necessarily. I've always done a lot of magazine pieces. What you do in the end is you just collect them together in a book. I mean, it's not as though you weren't writing a book when you do these pieces—look at my last book, *Music for Chameleons*, which was a best-seller and I sold two parts to the movies. It's actually all made up of pieces I had published in magazines.

And your other collection, The Dogs Bark, *as well.*

That's right.

Still, doesn't your journalism take second place in your mind to Answered Prayers?

Oh, nothing takes second place in my mind. Whatever I'm writing gets first place. I don't write on two different levels. I write on one level.

So you're able to put Answered Prayers *out of your mind when you're writing something else?*

Well, I'm thinking about it all the time.

If you're thinking about it, it's obviously not taking second place....

Somewhere inside of myself I'm thinking about it all the time.

In Breakfast at Tiffany's, *you characterized someone as having his nose pressed against the glass.*

Yes, looking in, seeing something that he wanted to be inside of.

Is that a good description of a writer: someone with his nose pressed against the glass?

Some writers.

Not your nose?

Some are sitting inside, looking out and saying, "What are those noses that are pressed against the glass? Oh, I do believe that's Gore Vidal's nose." (*Laughs.*)

Do you think that you have influenced American writing at all?

I know I've influenced American writing tremendously because of the influence I've had over writers in journalism. I mean, I invented those things, my dear. Other people go around collecting prizes for them. (*Laughs.*)

And will you be breaking new ground in future writings?

I already have. The pieces that I've published of *Answered Prayers* opened up a whole new field that's already been exploited beyond words. I mean, all these novels using famous people and whatnot.

Is journalism now the last great unexplored literary frontier?

I think so. But I think the two things are coming into a conjunction like two great rivers.

Fiction and nonfiction?

Yes. They're coming into a conjunction, divided by an island that is getting more and more narrow. The two rivers are going to suddenly flow together once and for all and forever. You see it more and more in writing.

With the difficulty being the possibility of lawsuits by the real-life characters?

I led the way and I'm not being sued too much. (*Laughs.*)

We'll get to your famous feud with Mr. Vidal, but let's stay with writing now. Do you think that Joyce and Proust took fiction as far as it could go?

Oh no, I don't at all. There is a root for fiction, but I think it's going to have to involve more and more what it is that I'm trying to do, which is to make truth into fiction, or fiction into truth—I don't know what it is, but it all has to do basically with truth treated in a fictional form.

But in your mind, fiction and nonfiction have blended together?

It's not really a matter of truth or nontruth. It is really a question of narrative writing, that's what it's really about. It's a question of learning to control the narrative so that it moves faster and deeper at the same time. Technically, I can maneuver just as well in both directions. The only thing that's easy for me to write is film scripts. There's a reason why. You assume you can write dialogue, take that for granted. The thing that's difficult about screenwriting and why there are so few well-known screenwriters, although there are many who are quite successful ones, is it's all construction. Once you have the thing constructed in your mind, scene by scene, how it will open and how it will end, the problem's solved. It's that construction that's so terribly difficult. And that's why strange people turn up very successful in Hollywood. You've never heard of them or anything, but they have that thing of being able to construct. I have a very good sense of construction. I construct backward. I always begin everything at the end and move backward toward the beginning. Well, it's always nice to know where you're going!

Does that mean you have to write with more insight in the beginning—when you're at the end—and decrease that insight as you work toward the beginning of the book?

Oh, I'm talking about when I'm constructing something and not when I'm actually writing. Although in the writing, I do always write the last chapter or the last few pages of a short story first.

How much influence has film had on your writing?

Per se, none.

Can you compare writing to the other arts, like to painting or music?

I think it's utterly separate.

In Music for Chameleons, *you wrote that you reread every word you ever published and came to the conclusion that you never in your writing life completely exploded all the energy and aesthetic excitements that material contained. You said you never worked with more than half, and sometimes a third, of the powers at your command. Do you still feel that way?*

I don't feel that way now. In fact, thinking it all back in retrospect, I think I was incorrect. When I said that, I was kind of self-hallucinating. I was not seeing things in a truthful way, because I certainly was, and always was, writing as well as I could. And my writing didn't change very vastly. As I've told you, I started writing when I was eight, and by the time I was sixteen I was really quite an accomplished writer. By the time I was seventeen, I started publishing. You go back to the earliest stories of mine and the style hasn't changed very much. The subject matter, of course, may be changed, but the actual style hasn't changed and the real reason for that is because of my ear. I write very much with my ear. I listen to the tone of language to a terrific extent and I have to be quite careful about this because every now and then I find myself using a word merely for the sound of it rather than for what it's really contributing to the thing. So I go through my manuscripts with a terrific amount of rewiting and crossing out.

James Joyce also wrote a great deal with his ear...

Too much so. In fact, I find Joyce a curious writer. I love his book of short stories, *Dubliners*. I think it's marvelous. Those stories he made are as good as anything I know in the English language. And yet, I've never liked another single thing of his.

Were you able to read Finnegans Wake?

No. I did read *Ulysses*, but I can't say that I did it with a great deal of pleasure. But I was fifteen or sixteen years old, perhaps I was too young.

You've said that all literature is ultimately gossip. Do you really believe that?

Of course. It's true.

Can you elaborate?

It's so obvious that I don't have to elaborate on it. All literature—from biographies to essays to novels to short stories—is gossip.

What was the gossip in Gulliver's Travels*?*

Well, he was commenting on the society of his time, in a way. It's just such an obvious thing. *Alice in Wonderland* is gossip. If you start to examine it, we get into incestuous gossip, then we get into the gossip of adults raping children. One could write an essay on *Alice in Wonderland* with Lewis Carroll, who turned out to be a total monster.

How can a writer use all he knows about writing in his work?

That was what I was trying to do with *Music for Chameleons*. By that, I was using all the different techniques I know about writing in one single piece, like those portraits that I did of people. I was using everything I know about prose writing, scriptwriting, all the different forms I've worked in, and applying all of the techniques simultaneously.

Does that, then, make it your best book?

No. But I think it's interesting because it worked a lot of the time.

Is the short story the hardest form of writing?

For the person who can really write it. Most people can't really write it, so it doesn't matter. But for the person who's a short-story artist it's the most difficult because it requires the greatest control and precision. Lots of writers write short stories, but they don't *write* short stories, so they don't know what they're doing.

Is Hemingway's "Big Two-Hearted River" the best American short story, in your opinion?

(*Laughs.*) Something must be going wrong in your brain somewhere.

That assessment has been attributed to you.

I said Hemingway wrote nine or ten very fine short stories and "Big Two-Hearted River" was one of them. Do I think it's the best or even *one* of the best American short stories? No. I don't think anything Hemingway did was one of the best of anything. There was a mean man.

Didn't he send you some kind of threatening letter after the publication of your first novel?

No. Well, I got a letter from him, a very rude letter too. But he did something even stranger than that. Nelson Algren, whom I did not know and never did know, published a book called *The Man with the Golden Arm*, and on the jacket of the book, larger than the title, larger in print than the author's name, was this blurb running across the top which said, "All you Capote fans, get your hats and get your coats, here comes a real writer," signed Ernest Hemingway. He mentioned me many times in little things that he wrote. He wrote an article in *The New York Times* which was ostensibly about baseball, but he used it to whack me in the head a couple of times. I don't know—I never met him.

Yet...

I couldn't stand him. Not because of that. I mean, before this ever happened. I disliked him. Everything about him.

You've called him dishonest and a "closet everything."

That he was a closet queen and everything else.

I guess I don't have to ask you to elaborate on that. But you've also said that you are secretly several of the things "the hairy one" pretended to be.

Well, I'm pretty tough.

I have a feeling you were saying more than that.

I can't think of anything that I meant, other than his whole kind of act that he put on. However, actually, I think that he was enormously vulnerable and sensitive in a way that I never thought of being. I'm sensitive about other people, but I'm not sensitive about myself.

Getting back to short-story writers, are there modern-day ones that you like, like John Cheever's stories

Yes, very good. Very fine short stories.

What about your former neighbor, Irwin Shaw?

Fabulous short-story writer, I think. I never liked any of his novels. I just don't really think that was his real form. But the short stories he wrote in the late thirties and early forties, like "Girls in Their Summer Dresses," really lovely. "Sailor off the Bremen." Very, very, very fine.

Norman Mailer has said that it would be hard to think of you ending a book badly. The first time you do, he believes, it will be because you've written your most adventurous book where you would be on to something large. Do you think he's right?

About me?

About you.

No.

Have you ever destroyed any manuscripts after completing them?

I destroyed an entire book that I wrote. It was a medium-length novel. Actually, it wasn't bad. It was highly publishable. It was about a New York debutante in the year of her being a debutante. And she was left alone by her family in their apartment in New York. The family goes to Europe on a vacation and she's left alone. Even the servants are gone on a holiday. And then the trouble she gets into in this apartment with the recklessness that's overcome her during the past year. It was quite a dramatic and very funny novel in part. It had a tragic end, though. But there was something about it that just bothered me. And recklessly one day, I destroyed it. I knew if I didn't, I would publish it. And I thought I'd rather not publish it.

Was that before or after Breakfast at Tiffany's?

It was after.

Was the character much different from Holly Golightly?

Oh yes, because she was very well educated and came from a totally different background than Holly.

Holly came from someone in real life.

Yes.

Did this girl as well?

Yes, mm-hmmm.

Do you have any other writings in drawers that haven't been published? That will one day be discovered? Short stories, profiles?

I have halves of stories, stories that I didn't finish that I maybe still will finish. I have a story about Malcolm Lowry, the man who wrote *Under the Volcano*. I knew him very well. I lived in Sicily a couple of years and he lived very near me. I would see a lot of him. He was a strange, hopeless, extraordinary sort of man and I wrote a long, long short story about him called "Another Day in Paradise." But I never have quite finished it. I never have put it all together and polished it. But that's a story I'm sure I will finish.

What did you think of him as a writer?

I thought he was very talented.

Do you think Under the Volcano *is a true classic?*

Underground classic. It's a very unusal work. I think it's a fascinating book and very beautiful.

Some consider that and Lawrence's The Plumed Serpent *the two best books about Mexico written by non-Mexicans.*

Yeah, I liked that too. The other book Lowry wrote had a rather beautiful title. It was called *Aquamarine.* No, not *aqua.* The name of it had to do with the changing colors of the sea. I can't think what the word could be, but I know *marine* is part of the word. You know, he was an alcoholic. He would come staggering up the path in the early afternoon already terribly drunk, sit on my terrace, and would want to talk. I would just have to keep on feeding him alcohol.

Was he writing then?

He would write when he was drinking. He was writing a book then which was never published. He used to give me things to read. He had more manuscripts—he must have had an absolute crate. He was writing a terrifically good book at that time. He didn't die till seven years after that. His health was terrible. I just remembered the name of his first novel. It's called *Ultramarine.* That's a lovely title. Don't you like it?

Yes. What other titles in literature do you really like?

Wuthering Heights, Pride and Prejudice, Gone With the Wind, Remembrance of Things Past, The Sun Also Rises, Look

Homeward, Angel, The Great Gatsby, Tender Is the Night, The Heart Is a Lonely Hunter, Other Voices, Other Rooms. (*Laughs.*) I think *Answered Prayers* is a good title.

Did anyone ever give you a title?

As a gift? No. No one ever actually has, that I can think of. Once someone turned a good story of mine into a great story. I gave it to them to read, one of the few times I was able to give something of mine to read to somebody before I published it. But this person's opinion I respected and I was interested in what they thought about such a curious story. And they said, "Just cut the last five lines out of this and you've got a great story." And it was true.

What was the story?

The story is called "Miriam." It's been in practically every collection. I just cut the last five lines and it turned a good story into really quite a great story.

That's what Ezra Pound did to T. S. Eliot's The Waste Land.

Oh yes, Pound did so much for him.

Do you like Eliot?

Never meant nothing to me. T. S. Eliot owes almost everything to Pound. I've never had anybody like that. I've never had anybody that I could show things to and ask their opinion.

What about Carson McCullers or some of the other writers you knew and respected? Did you ever exchange writings with any of them?

I showed Carson some things and she showed me *The Member of the Wedding* as it was being written. That was so long, it took her seven, eight years to write that.

Do you give advice, criticism? Or do you just read it and return it?

If I'm given it in that sense, I always give my opinion, what I think of it.

Do writers often send you things?

Yes.

Do you read them or return them unread?

If they're people unknown to me, I return the manuscript immediately with no comment or anything at all. Because I've known several people who've gotten into difficulties and problems by actually reading the manuscript or not reading it and not returning it and the person brings a lawsuit. I've had manuscripts sent to me that I haven't returned because they didn't put in an envelope to return them.

And then you get sued because you publish a story and they say you used their story.

You used their story. They'll sue you nowadays for absolutely nothing, and they can do it as we're talking about it—anybody can sue anybody for anything without it costing them a penny. But it costs you. Like my old case with Gore Vidal.

Which we'll get to. How do you feel about your name being used in the title of a novel, as Gordon Lish did with his book, Dear Mr. Capote?

Well, I've been through practically everything, so that's the least of it.

Have you made a lot of mistakes in your career? Like giving up the rights to your works?

Yes. In my opinion, I've made nothing but mistakes.

You once indicated that one learns more from failure than from success.

Yes, I think one *often* learns more from failure than success. Not always.

What have been the failures in your life that you've learned the most from?

Everything to do with the theater.

What did you finally learn—to stay away from it?

Virtually. (*Laughs.*) Everything surrounding the theater. It doesn't matter what you write, either. It's the things surrounding it—it's the producers, the people who invest in the plays, it's these nonentity fringe characters who enter into a whole artistic project, who really ought to be out selling bubble gum in front of Bloomingdale's. *They* make it impossible. I just find it impossible working in the theater. It takes an incredible time, an extraordinary energy and all of that going into it, and then going up in flames overnight because of some tiny mistake, something wrong with the lighting experts, something wrong with somebody's sore toe. I had enough of that. I was finished with it after the whole experience with *House of Flowers.* I spent so much time and effort—oh!

Wasn't it a production of a play of yours which brought you back from Europe after a long time abroad?

I left the country in 1947 and didn't come back for ten years. I might never have come back. I came back twice, once for a production of a play, *The Grass Harp.* And then I came back after I had lived a long time in Russia and I decided to go and do *In Cold Blood,* which meant a fantastic period of my life living in ghastly motels in the windswept plains of western Kansas on and off for six years—thank you, Norman Mailer! (*Laughs.*)

That's Gore and *now Norman we'll get back to. But since you mentioned living in Russia, didn't you write, in* The Muses Are Heard, *that the only people you could compare to the Russians were the Americans? What are the comparisons?*

Yes. They're very gregarious and outgoing. They're rather good-hearted. They drink too much. They're sentimental. I think Americans are quite sentimental, and certainly Russians are. That's about it.

What about the politicians of each country? Any similarities?

No. I mean, Russia is a county that doesn't *have* politics as we understand it. There are no elections. The people don't *run* as personalities. No Russian politician is out making a fool of himself like Mayor Koch, giving his interviews to *Playboy*, which cost him the governorship of New York. If Koch had not given that interview to *Playboy* magazine, he would have gotten the candidacy. The things he said in it were what caused him to lose the candidacy.

Do you think he feels that way as well?

I don't know. I don't know him.

How well did you know John Malcolm Brinnin, who wrote a long essay about you in his book Sextet?

He's never been a close friend of mine, he never really *was* a close friend of mine. I haven't seen him, to speak of, for twenty-five years.

Brinnin portrays you in your early years as a writer. He quoted you as saying about Faulkner that when you're reading him, you feel threatened by something in the back of your head that won't declare itself, "something maybe too close to home." Any truth in that?

No. That book of Mr. Brinnin's is very amusing. A great deal of untrue things are in it. I'd say seventy percent of what he wrote in it isn't true at all.

Really?

Well, he has all kinds of letters in there that I supposedly wrote him which I never wrote him at all.

So you obviously were not pleased with what he wrote.

Well, he wasn't accurate. I think *he* meant it to be very flattering. But he had a little trick in that book. There were these other people he wrote about, but the book is mostly about me.

The first ninety-six pages, anyway.

All through it. Whenever he wants to say something really unkind about somebody, he always says, "As Truman Capote said," etc. etc. He has a portrait of Cartier-Bresson in there. Well, I introduced him to Cartier-Bresson. That's about the limit of that, but he has me quoted throughout the piece as saying the most unkind and vicious things about Cartier-Bresson when, in fact, Cartier-Bresson has been a lifelong friend of mine and I've never said anything of the kind like that.

What were Brinnin's reasons, then?

'Cause *he* wanted to say these unkind things about Cartier-Bresson, because he didn't like him. But rather than say it himself he has *me* say it. You see, the strange thing about that book is that he so obviously thinks that he's being flattering to me. What's even stranger about it is that he's actually a good writer. He wrote that book which I thought was very good, called *Dylan Thomas in America.* But since reading this, I have to think back. I wonder just exactly how much of this *Dylan Thomas in America* was true.

What did you think of A. E. Hotchner's book on Hemingway, where he used a hidden tape recorder to get his quotes?

That was a piece of total junk. I mean, you can't scarcely be as bad a writer as A. E. Hotchner.

Have you ever used a tape recorder? Especially when researching In Cold Blood?

I never could have written *In Cold Blood* if (a) I had used a tape recorder or (b) I had ever taken a note. One of the earliest things I did was that piece on Brando—I never took one note. Then I spent sixteen hours writing it all out, nonstop, and put it away for about three months. Then I took it out, selected the things that I thought were relevant, that built toward the point I wanted to build, and that was it.

It was a beautiful piece.

I think so. I think it's one of the all-time perfect interviews.

It was truly a classic piece of journalism—and Brando was aware of it as well, which is probably what angered him and kept him from granting any in-depth interviews for over twenty years.

What angered him so much, according to him, was the scene with his mother at the end, which, when I was writing it, I knew was going to upset him, but I also knew it was the whole key to everything that I had done. If I didn't do the scene with the mother, it was just like I built a house and then lit a match and burned it down. Without that, everything that had gone before didn't make any sense. But if you understood where the passion and trouble of his youth had begun and how it ended... and I could make this connection with him because of my own mother, what had happened, and that I had had precisely the same experience and feeling, and I told him that, which is really the reason that he told me all of this about himself, and so I put it in, because I didn't feel it was any harm to his mother or any harm to him, I just felt it explained something about him sympathetically. I didn't realize it would upset him so because it wouldn't have upset me. That piece was essentially very sympathetic.

What he told me is basically what you've just said—that you came with a bottle of vodka under your arm and proceeded to tell him stories about yourself, which made him sympathetic and that's why he started to open up. But then when the piece appeared, all of your stories were gone and he felt tricked.

Yes, but you know perfectly well in doing an interview, the whole art is to leave yourself out of it. I did exactly the opposite in *Music for Chameleons* just to prove that you can do an interview with putting yourself in its center. But usually, the best thing to do is to leave yourself out of it.

(*When* Sayonara*'s director, Joshua Logan, heard that Capote wanted to come to Japan and write about Brando and the movie, he did all he could to stop him. He had read Capote's* New Yorker *piece on the American tour of Russia,* The Muses Are Heard, *and was not anxious to be Capote's next target.*

"The Muses Are Heard *was vicious and personally humiliating to everyone, especially Ira Gershwin and Leonard Lyons," Logan wrote in his book,* Movie stars, real people, and me. "*It treated human beings like bugs to be squashed underfoot. And Truman would have even juicier fodder to chew on with us. Boorish Hollywood invades Japan, and with golden ladies' man, Marlon Brando...*

"*...I called* The New Yorker *and complained vehemently. We also wrote letters through our lawyers. We said we would not cooperate and that Truman would be unwelcome on the set. But with all our protests, I had a sickening feeling that what little Truman wanted, little Truman would get.*

"*...Truman is dogged, ruthless, devious, and driven when he smells something sensational he can write about. And Marlon was his perfect pigeon."*

When "The Duke in His Domain" appeared, Logan's fears were realized. "It was just as bitchy as I had feared: it made us all into idiots.

"*...But the main part of Truman's piece was a cruel analysis* *of Marlon—every unfortunate detail, including his alcoholic mother and Marlon's various pretensions. Truman left nothing out.*

"I called Marlon about [it]. He was livid.

" 'That little bastard told me he wouldn't say any of the things I asked him not to and he printed them all. I'll kill him!' he shouted to me over the phone.

" 'It's too late, Marlon. You should have killed him before you invited him to dinner.' ")

What did Brando write to you after it appeared?

I don't really know, but he wrote me a very long single-spaced letter and I just honestly, truly don't remember what it was, but he was angry. I never save letters. It's a great pity, 'cause I've had some fantastic letters. But everything goes down the incinerator.

You must get a great deal of mail. Do you read all the things that are sent to you?

I don't read them. I don't even open them. They're stacked in my apartment at this moment, ready to go down the incinerator. I lose lots of checks that way because the checks are in the envelopes from the Dramatists Guild, this, that, and the other thing. But I'd rather lose checks than begin to try to go through them. Every now and then I'll thumb through a whole bunch of letters. Something about a handwriting, something will tell me that this is something different. And I'm usually right.

What is it about the handwriting?

There's something about it that's intelligent, something about it that tells you that somebody who is really a person has written a letter.

Have you *ever written about people to their satisfaction?*

You must know as well as I do that that is an impossibility. (*Laughs.*) It is *totally* impossible. Unless you're working for a greeting card company.

How close were you with the critic Newton Arvin?

Very.

He felt that you had something in common with Hawthorne and Melville—a sense of evil. Do you know what he meant by that?

I didn't know that Newton thought that. I know that he thought I had something in common with Hawthorne. I don't think he thought I had anything in common with Melville. He wrote the only good book ever written about Melville.

Nothing to do with evil?

Not that I know of.

What did he think you had in common with Hawthorne?

It had to do with subject matter and atmosphere. Hawthorne wrote a beautiful short story, it's not one of his most famous, but it's really beautiful, called "The Minister's Black Veil," and Newton always used to say that my work reminded him so much of "The Minister's Black Veil," that he would swear that either I had stolen it from Hawthorne or Hawthorne had stolen it from me, in some reincarnation in the past.

Didn't Cocteau once tell Colette that you were ageless and had a very wicked mind?

Yes.

How acute was he?

I don't know. I knew Cocteau quite well. When I knew him best I was about twenty-one years old. You see, I always looked very much younger than I was when I was in my twenties. I looked about fifteen or fourteen years old. So, when Cocteau first met me, he thought that I was about fourteen.

How old was he?

It was 1947. I guess he must have been in his late fifties. And he thought the way that I talked and the way that I was and how I wrote and everything—he had a great friend called Raymond Radiguet, a famous French writer who died when he was only twenty-three years old. A brilliant young writer. And he thought that I was very like Raymond Radiguet. He thought Raymond had a great sense of *vivre* and he'd say, "You're just like Raymond."

Well, how wicked is your mind?

I don't think I have a wicked mind at all. I just have a double sense of perception. I sort of see what's good and I see what's bad simultaneously.

Do you see more bad than good?

Well, truth be known, I think there's more bad than there is good so, naturally, I've seen more bad than good. But I see quite a good deal of good here and there.

You've admitted to committing some serious sins, deliberate cruelty among them. Can you go into that?

I don't know. You see, I just write these things out of my mind.

And then someone like me comes along, having read what you've written, and asks, "What does that mean?"

I just write them out of my mind. When they find your body floating facedown in the river tomorrow, they'll wonder.

Do you think, though, that you are a cruel person?

No.

What do you think of Mark Twain's statement—

Now *he* was evil!

Why was Mark Twain evil?

I think it's wonderful that he wrote *Tom Sawyer* and *Huckleberry Finn* and he had one of the more wicked minds ever going. He wrote one of the most pornographic books ever published in America, except that it was never really distributed. I've forgotten what it was called. But he wrote a lot of very strange things.

He said that man is the most detestable of all creatures.

I had that quoted in my book, *Handcarved Coffins.*

You quoted it a few times.

Mm-hmmm. I think it's true. There's no other living creature that's as wicked as man. I mean, animals never do the detestable, horrible things that human beings do. Can you imagine animals creating concentration camps and torturing people to death? Or, for that matter, can you imagine animals with a capital-punishment law running through the gorilla family?

Do you think that man will ever change?

No.

Will we become more and more corrupt? Will the world become more totalitarian? Are we heading toward that?

I don't know. I think something's going to happen. I think the world's getting overly populated. Something's going to happen in the twenty-first century. Everything's going to change, and so drastically that I'm not quite sure what it is. I feel as though the whole world is all going to become one for once. I mean, there aren't going to be any countries. I feel there's going to be a terrific war. I don't know when. There's going to be a great depopulation in the world, and from that is going to arise an entirely different kind of civilization than we know today.

Do you feel that the works of art and the culture that we have preserved will last or disappear?

There'll always be museums. Museums of the spirit, museums of the canvases. But I do feel that there's going to be some drastic change. I don't feel that it's very rapidly coming, but I think, within the next hundred years as we look back at today, we're going to be quite amazed.

Are you happy to have lived at this time, or is there any other period when you would have preferred to live?

I would have preferred to live in the eighteenth century.

In what country?

I would have preferred to live in France and been very rich.

5

In Cold Blood

"Everybody has their field. My field is the multiple murderer."

Capote never claimed—as many critics thought he did—that he invented narrative journalism or, as *In Cold Blood* came to be labeled, the nonfiction novel. He *did* consider it to be a serious new literary form and he did feel he had made a major contribution toward its establishment. And he also staked the claim to have undertaken the most comprehensive and far-reaching experiment in the medium of reportage.

When he began his investigation into the murder of the Clutter family in Holcomb, Kansas, Perry Smith and Richard Hickock had not yet been apprehended. Once they were, Capote needed their cooperation before he could write his book. He got more than he bargained for. "Short of actually living in a death cell myself," he said, "I couldn't have come closer to their experience."

He spent long hours with them as they waited to be hanged; he shared their emotions. It was a life totally alien to anything he had ever undergone, and he told *Playboy*,

"I came to understand that death is the central factor of life. And the simple comprehension of this fact alters your entire perspective. . . .

"The experience served to heighten my feeling of the tragic view of life, which I've always held and which accounts for the side of me that appears extremely frivolous; that part of me is always standing in a darkened hallway, mocking tragedy and death. That's why I love champagne and stay at the Ritz."

In Music for Chameleons *you quoted a line from Henry James: "We live in the dark, we do what we can, the rest is the madness of art." The line impressed you and you later describe yourself sitting alone in your dark madness. How dark and how mad is it?*

What I meant by that was, for instance, in a book like *In Cold Blood*, which took me six years to write, I know a writer has to be alone a good deal of the time and, as I've told you, at one point I spent seven months on a mountain in Switzerland virtually isolated, not seeing anyone, writing or working on that book—and the subject matter and the loneliness led to a definite darkness and terrific apprehension. I've never been so nervous and so agitated. I never slept more than three hours a night for the seven months there.

What was it that led to such agitation? Was it the solving of the problems of the book or was it the reliving of what had happened to Hickock and Smith and the Clutter family?

It's just very difficult to write. It's difficult for anyone to write, but I find it *extremely* difficult. I'd just as soon have not been a writer if I'd had a choice.

But you've never had a choice?

No, not really.

What about your choice of subject matter? Was it the idea of writing about a gruesome murder which attracted you to writing In Cold Blood*?*

I didn't choose that subject because of any great interest in it. It was because I wanted to write what I called a nonfiction novel—a book that would read exactly like a novel except that every word of it would be absolutely true. I had written a book that was like that called *The Muses Are Heard.* It was a short book about Russia and every word of it was true and it reads like a short novel, but I wanted to do it on a grand scale. I had two sort of dry runs with subjects that just turned out not to have enough material in them to do what I wanted to do and finally I settled on this obscure crime in this remote part of Kansas because, I felt, if I followed this from beginning to end it would provide me with the material to really accomplish what was a technical feat. It was a literary experiment where I was choosing a subject not because of a great attraction to the subject, because that was not true, but because it suited my purposes literarily speaking.

Yet, you weren't able to remain detached once you got involved in the story of the murders; did you find yourself being sucked into the story almost against your will?

Yes, because I became so totally involved in it personally that it just took over and consumed my life. All the trials, the appeals, the endless research I had to do—something like eight thousand pages of pure research—and my involvement with the two boys who had committed the crime. Everything. It was a matter of living with something day in and day out. That's why I have no respect for Norman Mailer's book *The Executioner's Song*, which, as far as

I'm concerned, is a nonbook. He didn't live through it day by day, he didn't know Utah, he didn't know Gary Gilmore, he never even *met* Gary Gilmore, he didn't do an ounce of research on the book—two other people did all of the research. He was just a rewrite man like you have over at the *Daily News.* I spent six *years* on *In Cold Blood* and not only knew the people I was writing about, I've known them better than I've known *anybody.* So Mailer's book just really *annoyed* me. Can you see why it annoyed me?

Sure, but when you read his book, couldn't you appreciate the fact that he was even able to do it?

No! I was so annoyed by the whole thing about the book. I didn't like the book, I didn't like his attitude about the characters, I didn't like his point of view, I didn't like the writing... but most of all, I didn't like the fact he hadn't done it!

Well, it's true he had help with the research, but he did actually write the book. Do you feel that without your book he wouldn't have been able to do his?

No, he never would have. Norman and I were quite good friends until the last year or two. And now I don't feel friendly toward Norman *at all.* He said something to me on a television program to the effect that I had criticized him on his book *The Executioner's Song* as being a copycat. Well, Norman *has* been copying me for years, but it started back with *The Muses Are Heard.* Norman didn't understand my whole feeling about nonfiction narrative writing, he never understood what I was talking about. I remember an extremely violent conversation with him when I was in the middle of writing *In Cold Blood* because he told me it was a failure of the imagination which caused me to have this extreme drive in this direction. I said, "It's exactly the opposite. It's imagination that's causing me to *have* the drive!" But this television thing brought it up. Well, in the introduction in *Music for Chameleons* I said, but very lightly and very jokingly, that I was so glad to be of such help to Norman Mailer. It really was meant as a joke but he brought it up and said that I had said things in interviews about him. I actually never had, up to that point. As a matter of fact, up to *this* point.

Mailer says he feels guilty about saying certain things about you, especially when he was quoted as saying your life was wrecked, not very long ago. He said it was a journalist who led him down that garden path to get a provocative quote.

How do you know that Norman feels guilty about saying those things about me?

He told me. I did an interview with him for cable television. He said that the reason he didn't publicly acknowledge In Cold Blood *when he published his book was because he felt that your book was so famous that everyone would know it.*

That's what he said to me on television. That's ridiculous. I mean, I acknowledged the fact that why I wrote *The Muses Are Heard* was because of Lillian Ross's *Picture*. I wanted to see if I did it using all the techniques of a fiction writer, but I certainly mentioned Lillian Ross over and over. Without her, I don't think it really would have occurred to me at that point. It would have occurred to me later because I was doing it all the time, but not on a very large scale. Lillian did a wonderful job. She's a very good reporter, but she's not a very good writer in the sense that we're talking about. She just doesn't have the *lift*—that final, dreadful thing that it takes. There's a moment in writing when it's either going to really lift or it's not.

Is it usually within the first seventy-five pages?

Not necessarily. I read Norman's book *Ancient Evenings* and it never lifted once.

Did you read the whole thing?

Most of it. It never even got off the page anywhere.

He says it's the best writing he's ever done.

I can understand *why* he said that. He feels on the defensive. But he's written far better things than that.

What of his work do you like?

Norman's book that I liked best was *Advertisements for Myself*. There was good writing in it and it was more truthful and honest and more like what's best about him. I never liked his fiction, but I've liked his nonfiction. I thought *Armies of the Night* was quite a good book.

What about his book on Marilyn Monroe?

Oh, that was so ridiculous it isn't worth discussing. I, at least, have the courtesy to ignore what is so obviously insane. Norman sits down to ostensibly write a reasonably short book and he ends up writing *Gone With the Wind* about somebody he never even knew. Marilyn was a great friend of mine and I wrote a piece about her that was really a wonderful piece—"A Beautiful Child"—but he never even met Marilyn. It was that same guy [Lawrence Schiller] who put him up to that as put him up to *The Executioner's Song*. Well, I can understand that Norman needs the money, but...

(What Norman Mailer actually said when I told him that Capote said—long before Ancient Evenings *was published—that* Ancient Evenings *couldn't possibly be a good book because Mailer was only good at writing about what he knew and he didn't know anything about ancient Egypt, any more than he knew about Gary Gilmore or Marilyn Monroe, was: "Well, Truman's very upset about* The Executioner's Song. *He feels that I should*

have made a pilgrimage and gotten down on my knees and said, 'Oh, great Cardinal Capote, do I have your blessing? May I proceed to write a book about a killer?' And I didn't. He went around saying, 'He never gave any credit to In Cold Blood.' *Well, I just thought that book was so famous that you didn't have to give credit to it. Anyone assumed that I did* The Executioner's Song *having* In Cold Blood *in mind. But I reread* In Cold Blood *after I finished* The Executioner's Song *and it's a very good novel. It's probably as much of a novel as* The Executioner's Song. *Maybe more. And it's very nicely written. And it may end up being a classic because it is something that is remarkable. But I don't know what he's talking about, it just sort of struck me as kind of a dumb remark. Truman is canny as hell, but he's not the brightest guy in the world.")*

If you ever tackled a long investigative piece like In Cold Blood *again, would you follow Mailer's route and hire researchers?*

Never. I think that is so unbelievable.

Malcolm Cowley, among others, took exception to your claim that you had invented the nonfiction novel—pointing out that Henry Adams did this in 1907 when he wrote The Education of Henry Adams *and Hemingway did it with* Green Hills of Africa *in 1935.*

That's not true. I don't know about Henry Adams but I know *Green Hills of Africa*, which is nothing but a kind of autobiographical travel piece. And, in any event, he has himself in it all the time. The great accomplishment of *In Cold Blood* is that I never appear once. There's never an *I* in it at all.

So there's no doubt in your mind that you achieved literary history with that book?

Yes, I did. Just look at the multitude of copycats.

Have any of them surpassed what you've done?

No.

Do any of them get close?

Not that I've read.

You've spoken of the experience of writing In Cold Blood *as being too painful, saying nothing was worth it. In retrospect, do you still feel that way?*

Well, I certainly wouldn't do it again. If I knew or had known when I started it what was going to be involved, I never would have started it, regardless of what the end result would have been.

How close did you get to the death-row experiences of Dick Hickock and Perry Smith?

What do you mean, get to it?

To what it was actually like. You were there. You saw the hangings. It affected you. I believe you've said that you vomited from it.

It was the most emotional experience of my creative life, yes.

And of your personal life?

No.

You've talked about their stark and brutal conversations with you—

I don't remember *talking* about it.

Mentioning that they were stark and brutal, anyway. Were you the last person to speak with them?

Yes, I was the *very* last person to speak to them.

Have you ever talked about what they said to you?

Well, they just wished me good-bye. (*Pauses.*) Perry said to me, "Good-bye. I love you and I always have." Perry Smith.

And how did you react to that?

Well, I was standing there at the foot of the gallows. There were about fifty people surrounding me. They couldn't hear what he said to me because he was whispering. I was very upset.... But I was upset terrifically about the whole thing. That was just the straw that was a little too heavy.

Did you reciprocate that love in any way? Did you feel you loved either of them, after being so close and intimate with them?

I didn't love either one of them, but I had a great understanding for both of them, and for Perry I had a tremendous amount of sympathy. Dick, I thought, was just a small-time crook who got into water way over his head and was really responsible for this whole murder, which Perry actually committed. But Perry would not have committed it if he hadn't been led on in what the French call a *folie à deux.*

Although they so cold-bloodedly murdered a family of four, you didn't think they should have been killed, did you?

No. I'm very much against capital punishment. But I've seen a number of people executed.

Is it something that you are attracted to see, as a writer?

No, I did it as research. I saw two people executed after Perry and Dick. I was going to write a thing about executions and about my feelings against capital punishment, which I actually never wrote. I've written it in my journal, but I've never done a piece about it.

You've spent a considerable amount of time interviewing killers, haven't you?

Most of the interviews I did during the ten years I went into and out of *In Cold Blood.* Since then I've only done about a hundred and seven interviews. Maybe more. I could kill that Whizzer White for what he did with that man who was being executed in Texas. They put the needle in his arm and darling little Whizzer White was waiting until they were shooting the juice into his arm to bother to telephone and say, "Well, let's just hold this off." I mean, that's just such a terrible level of tragedy. The man has to go through it over again, he should have been left alone. That's one person I really despise, Byron White. I follow the Supreme Court very closely. I began to twenty years ago when I first became so involved in crimes and I began to follow the Supreme Court and their decisions and I have an opinion about every one.

Is there any Justice on the Supreme Court you respect?

The only person at the moment on the Supreme Court whose grave I wouldn't spit on is Brennan. The rest of them, I would spit on their graves. Except the lady. She hasn't been on there long enough—although I have followed her decisions and I don't think she's been too bright.

Sandra O'Connor seems to be a very conservative woman.

Yes. She hasn't done anything that you can make any particular judgment about her. But the person who is a real hypocrite and who is not only *conservative* but is a cruel person is Byron White.

Do you know any of the Supreme Court justices personally?

I guess I've met them all, except I haven't seen any of them in the last five years.

Who would you like to see on the Supreme Court?

I don't know. I'd like to see the whole Supreme Court change.

In what ways?

I think they should have something like the Soviet Politburo.

Isn't that just a bit radical?

I don't believe in the Supreme Court as it is. I don't believe the setup is right. I don't believe that the Supreme Court is large enough.

Should it have twice as many justices?

Yes. At least. It's too small a group handling too much, trying to do more than it's possible for any group of people to do. I know they don't have the time and they have too many cases. If they double the Supreme Court, it doesn't mean that the whole court has to decide each issue. They can be divided. Some cases are obviously so much more important than others. The whole court should decide once and for all on the death penalty, which they keep avoiding and avoiding and avoiding. That whole thing with the death sentence is one of the most serious issues in American life, although it may seem minor, in a way. But it isn't. And the fact that there are twelve hundred and seventy people on death row waiting day and night to know whether they're going to be executed is absolutely outrageous beyond words. Just because the Supreme Court can't make up its mind one way or the other.

If they made up their mind and voted for the death penalty...

Then I think they should carry out the executions and stop this torture.

One of the more infamous prisoners you know is Charles Manson. How well do you know him?

I know him, but I don't know him all that well. But I don't want to know him, I hate him.

Didn't you know four of the five people who were killed in the Sharon Tate house?

Yes. Isn't it fabulous?

You don't think, though, that Manson was the mastermind behind that little band of crazies, do you?

No, Bobby Beausoleil was.

You met him in San Quentin prison and he was apparently impressed that you walked freely in the yard. Is it dangerous for you to walk around in prison yards?

I don't feel it is. Prisoners think that it is. Bobby Beausoleil said, "Somebody will kill you just to get their name in the papers."

What about Sirhan Sirhan. You've known him...

...A long time.

And do you think he should be released?

Oh...yes.

Why?

Because he certainly would never kill anybody again. I don't think he should have been in prison in the first place. He should have been in a hospital for treatment for a few years. He's a harmless little toad. I don't have any sympathy for him at all, but I don't think there's any point keeping him in prison. It's just a gesture to do so.

Do you think that Robert Kennedy would have been President if he hadn't been killed?

No. I despised Kennedy.

Besides Sirhan Sirhan, you also knew Lee Harvey Oswald and *both Jack and Bobby Kennedy, didn't you?*

Yeah, isn't that fabulous?

Are you the only person in the world who can make that connection?

I only know one other person who knew both Jack Kennedy and Lee Harvey Oswald, a girl called Priscilla Johnson, who worked for U.P. in Moscow. That's the only other person in the world that knew both of them.

What is your opinion of Oswald?

Highly neurotic. Certainly crazy. I only saw him twice. I'd say my total encounter with him altogether would add up to about five hours.

Where were your encounters?

In Moscow, just when he defected. I was living in Moscow.

Do you think he acted alone?

Oh, yes.

So, there's no conspiracy in your mind. What about Martin Luther King, Jr.? Again, single killer?

Mm-hmmm. I think it's very strange they're making this legal holiday, because I don't think they know the truth (*laughs*) about Martin Luther King.

And you do?

Well, Martin Luther King had many sides. (*Laughs.*)

There's a devilish twinkle in your eye—what sides do you *know about?*

Nothing that nobody doesn't know. I think everybody knows.

Do you think he was a great man at all?

Oh, yes, mm-hmmm. I think he's just fine. (*Laughs.*)

Getting back to the men on death row—is a lot of your mail letters from these condemned men?

I guess I get more mail from death-penalty prisoners than anybody. I certainly get an awful lot. There's scarcely a literate person on death row who hasn't written me at one time or another.

Is it always the same? Some kind of plea for help?

They want me to write something about their case.

Are they all innocent, in their minds?

Ah-hah. Or, at least they don't feel that their case has been presented by the media in a true light. Like this John Gacy. Did I tell you about him?

No.

He isn't saying, "I didn't murder the thirty-three people," but that his whole case has been misrepresented to the public, which turns out to be absolutely true. To give you a simple example: the way his case was presented to the public was that he was a sort of child molester who got fourteen-year-old boys and raped and murdered them. Not one word of that is true, not at all. All of his victims were between ages seventeen and twenty-eight and all of them were whores. They were boys who would walk a particular stretch of park in Chicago where cars just circulate around and around picking them out as they choose. And almost every single one of the victims came from that particular thing. He'd just drive his car around until he finally would pick out a boy and take him home and have sex with him and then murder him. Now, the thing that was wrong in the way the media addressed it was you would think he was taking innocent little high-school kids and doing this instead of really tough ones who were being paid twenty-five dollars for whatever it was that they did. But the thing that was strange to me about the case is why—having, in a sense, not committed any kind of crime at all in his sexual relationship—why did he murder them? I mean, it wasn't as though they were what the papers made it sound like.

Did you talk to him? Did you ask him?

I asked him that question and it was the last I heard from him. He didn't want to answer that question.

Wasn't he a man who was struggling with his homosexuality? He would have sex with them but then kill them because he was depressed by it?

I don't think that that was it. I don't know what the answer is.

Couldn't there have been a part of himself that hated what he was doing sexually and so he felt he had to kill that part? Isn't that one reason a killer kills?

Maybe you've got the answer . . . but I think the killing was part of the pleasure. I don't think it came about because of any sense of guilt or retribution. I've talked to many a strangler. They get a curious pleasure out of it, like the awful thing with children who strangle a cat. You know, they get some terrible, awful sensations from it.

Is that the case with all stranglers, you think?

I think definitely with stranglers. Stranglers get a pleasure out of killing.

Isn't that supposedly true with killers who use a knife as well? That they get a great deal of pleasure sticking the knife in?

That's what they say.

It isn't easy sticking a knife in deep enough to kill, is it? You have to really push to get it in.

They say it's very easy, the few people who will talk about it. So few of them are ever willing to talk to you about what they actually do and how they feel. The few that have actually been willing to talk to me about what they feel about knifing, they get a real pleasure from the actual feel of the knife going into the body. For instance, that Jack Abbott, in his book, described this thing of how it felt pushing the knife into somebody, knowing just where to put it under the ribs, seeing the expression on the person's face . . .

Why do murderers almost always laugh when discussing their crimes?

I think they feel a sudden rush of embarrassment. You know, what's called an embarrassed laugh? That's how I would describe it. It comes over them despite whatever their mentality is. They feel suddenly a sense of shame.

You feel that murderers do *feel a sense of shame about their crimes?*

Oh, yes. That's why they find it so difficult to talk about it.

Have you ever wondered why you are able to relate so well to murderers?

Because right away they realized that I wasn't passing any judgment on them. I had no opinion about them as a person regarding the fact that they'd killed or no matter what their crime had been, because I don't.

I know magazines have asked you to write about the multiple murderer. Why haven't you?

I started one particular piece. It was called "Darker Corridors: Opinions on the Mind of the Multiple Murderer." But I'm not sure I'm going to finish it. I certainly have my opinions on the mind of the multiple murderer. I knew over four hundred of them. Everybody has their field. My field is the multiple murderer.

Is there anything they all have in common?

I'm not going to go into that now. There is one thing that eighty percent of them have in common, and it's the only thing I'll tell you. Eighty percent of multiple murderers have tattoos. Interview after interview after interview, the person always turned out to be tattooed, either a little bit or a lot.

So when you see someone with a tattoo, stay away?

You should do that for a lot of reasons. There's something really the matter with most people who wear tattoos. There's at least some terrible story. I know from experience that there's always something terribly flawed about people who are tattooed, above some little something that Johnny had done in the Navy, even though that's a bad sign.

What about the Japanese who are tattooed from head to foot? Is that a whole other thing?

It's terrible. Psychologically it's crazy. Most people who are tattooed, it's the sign of some feeling of inferiority, they're trying to establish some macho identification for themselves.

Have you known many Jewish multiple murderers with tattoos?

They're rarer than most. Not as gangsters, Jewish gangsters are just as prevalent as Italian gangsters.

Did you know that a Jew with a tattoo cannot be buried in a Jewish cemetery?

I didn't know that. (*Pauses, thinking.*) That's fascinating. I'm glad you told me that. I wish I had known that a long time ago.

Do most multiple murderers believe in God, or are they atheists?

They all believe in God.

Do they have a sense of shame or remorse about what they've done?

That's where it's very hard, very difficult, because it's so hard to get them to talk about what they did and what they feel about it. There's the real turning point. I can know a person for years, talk to them any number of times, know every single thing in their lives, about the first time they ever masturbated, and they're not able to rise to the occasion to acknowledge that they really did kill their mother, father, brother, and two sisters.

How long does it take a murderer to feel comfortable enough around you for him to open up to you?

It depends on the person. After I get to know them, usually they like to talk, because they don't have anybody to talk to.

Do they always know who you are?

Oh yes.

Most of them have read In Cold Blood?

Yes, that's how I get the interviews.

How many of them may have read your work before *they killed?*

I don't know. (*Pauses.*) I haven't thought about that.

6

Contemporaries

> "I don't feel in competition with other writers. Because I don't write about the same things as any other writer that I know of does."

Age has a way of hardening opinions. When Capote was younger, he was willing to call Norman Mailer "commendable" and say that he thought John Updike was "a gifted fellow" who could write "beautifully" ("although he doesn't write *about* anything"). In his *Playboy* interview he generously admitted that "Bernard Malamud and Saul Bellow and Philip Roth and Isaac Bashevis Singer and Norman Mailer are all fine writers, but they're not the *only* writers in the country, as the Jewish literary Mafia would have us believe."

Two of those writers went on to win the Nobel Prize and Mailer received two Pulitzers—the kind of recognition Capote never got. Other than those three O. Henry awards, he was given the Mystery Writers of America Edgar Allan Poe Award in 1966 and an Emmy Award for television adaptation in 1967, but he felt he deserved more.

In his *Paris Review* interview, Capote said, "I've never

been aware of direct literary influence, though several critics have informed me that my early works owe a debt to Faulkner and Welty and McCullers. Possibly. I'm a great admirer of all three; and Katherine Anne Porter, too."

One of those critics, his old nemesis Gore Vidal, was a bit harsher in *his* 1969 *Playboy* interview: "Neither Mailer nor Capote nor myself—to name three writers of very different gifts—came into his own until he found his proper voice. Mailer spent years trying to write timeless masterpieces, and the time of that time was disastrous for him. Capote was not quite so ambitious—or literary. He simply wanted to be famous through writing, and so he copied the works of writers who were currently in fashion. He plundered Carson McCullers for *Other Voices, Other Rooms*, abducted Isherwood's Sally Bowles for *Breakfast at Tiffany's*; in short, was ruthlessly unoriginal. Then he turned to reportage, the natural realm of those without creative imagination, and began to do interesting work. In other words, he'd found his own voice, and that is what writing is all about."

And in a *Paris Review* interview in 1974, Vidal answered a question concerning Capote's expertise at promoting his books with the comment: "Every writer ought to have at least one thing that he does well, and I'll take Truman's word that a gift for publicity is the most glittering star in his diadem."

Of course, Capote was well-known for giving at least as much as—and probably more than—he had to take. As a youth, he acknowledged, he developed the muscles of a barracuda in the art of dealing with one's enemies. In talking about his contemporaries, he stretches those muscles and bares his teeth.

CONTEMPORARIES

You've referred to the "subtle but savage" difference between very good writing and true art. Can you distinguish between the two by using examples of writers you admire?

Thackeray's a good writer and Flaubert is a great artist. Trollope is a good writer and Dickens is a great artist. Colette is a very good writer and Proust is a great artist.

Can you move up to more current examples?

Katherine Anne Porter was an extremely good writer and Willa Cather was a great artist. (*Pauses.*) I can't think of anyone just offhand at the moment that I think is a great artist today.

William Faulkner said that a good writer must be completely ruthless. Are you?

Well, *he* was completely reckless. I'm not a great admirer of Faulkner. He never had the slightest influence on me at all. I like three or four short stories of his, "That Evening Song," and I like one novel of his very much, called *Light in August.* But for the most part, he's a highly confusing, uncontrolled writer. He doesn't fit into my category of the kind of writer I really respect. I knew Faulkner very well. He was a great friend of mine. Well, as much as you could be a friend of his, unless you were a fourteen-year-old nymphet. Then you could be a great friend!

Has any American writer had an influence on you as a writer?

No American writer has.

You've always believed that style, more than content, is the mirror of an artist's sensibility. Are the great writers more concerned with style or content?

That's an impossible thing to answer. Flaubert is a great writer and a great stylist. He was more concerned with style than content. Content with him was like he would take an apple out of a basket and put it on a table and say, "Now I'm going to do this apple." I mean, I don't think he really gave a fuck about Madame Bovary. He cared how it all shaped itself, how real he could make it. He was a great stylist. It's strange about Flaubert because he could do such beautiful, fantastic things and then he could do something dreadful, like *Petrochette* or *Popachette* or whatever that last book was called. So bad. So, I don't know. ... Henry James is a total stylist.

Wasn't Faulkner, as well?

Faulkner was not a stylist. Faulkner just fell into a kind of sloppy style, over which he had no real control. He was writing about something. Now, his thing was content. He fell into a style, but it was by mistake and it wasn't a good style.

What about Dostoyevsky? He seemed more concerned with content. He didn't seem to be much of a stylist.

Yes he is. He's a *lousy* stylist. (*Laughs.*)

Can you read Russian?

Not that well to make that opinion, but I can read it a bit.

And how is he in Russian?

Terrible. Turgenev is a stylist.

What about Gertrude Stein? Did you know her?

No. I knew Alice Toklas.

What did you think of the two of them?

I thought they made a great Mutt-and-Jeff team. (*Laughs.*)

What's your opinion of Stein as a writer?

I liked her book about Alice. But as for the rest of Gertrude... "I am a pot of shit, I am a pot of shit, I am a pot of shit..." (*Laughs.*)

What do you think of her idea of repetition—it was a very conscious thing with her.

It's a way of filling up the page. Maybe if you'd space it.

Have you ever tried reading The Making of Americans?

Yes. I got nowhere.

Let's talk about more contemporary stylists. What do you think of Thomas Pynchon?

Ghastly.

Have you read his work?

Yes, I'm one of the few people in the world who has actually read *Gravity's Rainbow* from page one to the last page, since I was a judge on the National Book Awards in which it was being considered. It didn't win because of me. Actually, several other people wanted to vote for that awful other writer who I can't stand, Donald Barthelme. He's the most boring, fraudulent writer.

How did he become so popular then?

He began at *The New Yorker.*

Still, his style has influenced college students much the way Hemingway did years ago.

I hope you're not telling me the truth, because I cannot stand Donald Barthelme, and I haven't seen anyone who writes remotely like him.

What about Tom Wolfe?

I like Tom Wolfe, but I think he's extremely uneven. He's written some wonderful things. That piece he did about the people going to Leonard Bernstein's party—*Radical Chic*—that is really a marvelous piece of modern reportage. When he's swinging with it and not getting too full of chicklets, he's amusing. I wouldn't mind that, except for his own sake. I know it's going to die. That's why, myself, I always stick to a strictly classic writing style, where everything is timeless. Nothing is going to date it—not the quality of the writing, not the subject. I always felt very strongly about that, and it's hard to do, it's hard to know what it is you're doing. Tom Wolfe is just not going to last. I love some of the things he's done, they're just terrific... but you won't think so in years to come. Because of his style. But if he hadn't used that style, nobody would have paid attention to him and he wouldn't have had the success that he had. But *Candy-Colored Cadillac*...

You mean The Kandy-Kolored Tangerine-Flake Streamline Baby.

Whatever.

What do you think of Hunter Thompson?

I don't know if he's a copycat of Tom Wolfe. I'm quite sure that Tom Wolfe is not a copycat of him. But I wonder how much he's been influenced by Tom Wolfe. In any event, he has written three or four things that are as good as Tom Wolfe, if not better. But he's even *more* uneven. But the three or four things that he's done that are terrific, nobody has ever seemed to read them, like the piece he did about going to the Kentucky Derby. That was absolutely fabulous. *(Laughs.)* And that other one about being on that political train with one of the politicians. He was carrying Tom Wolfe's thing one step further, but he's a writer who's already dead.

And Ken Kesey?

Well, he's dead. I mean, he only wrote that one book. He was a victim of the same kind of... If one didn't know better, one would believe that all three of those writers were raised in the same orphanage in Los Angeles. *(Laughs.)*

There's another stylist I've been meaning to ask you about: Jack Kerouac. I know you dismissed him in your now famous remark to Norman Mailer on a TV show, when Mailer praised Kerouac and you said, "That's not writing, that's typewriting." Still, he was a force for a while and—

Jack Kerouac? He was a joke, what are you talking about?

Did you read On the Road?

Of course I read it.

The book did usher in an era.

Joke, joke, joke.

Well, then, how many writers are just typing?

Ninety-nine-point-nine percent. *(Laughs.)* And that's being generous. Poor old Jack Kerouac.

What's your opinion of the so-called "black humorists," like Donleavy, Southern, Heller...

I don't like any of them.

Have you ever read Donleavy's The Ginger Man?

Yeah, I didn't like it. I read it in the Olympia Press edition.

Apparently that's a very valuable edition.

I have it somewhere in my subterranean cellar.

Joseph Heller's Catch-22 *was another pacesetting book.*

To tell the honest truth, I really don't have any opinion about him at all, because I never could read *Catch-22*. It bored me. It's just not my kind of thing, not my kind of writing. The very subject matter itself was something I don't like. I don't like anything to do with the *militaire*, generally speaking. But I'm glad he's recovering from his very dangerous illness that he had. He had a horrible disease that's worse than that thing called Lou Gehrig disease and he was just dissolved and falling apart. And he had a remission from it and he's apparently recovering and is able to function.

What do you think about Nabokov?

I like Nabokov. I think Nabokov was an artist.

What modern writer, in your opinion, writes the best sentences?

Prose writers? E. M. Forster—beautiful, beautiful prose writer. Marvelous paragraphs he wrote.

What about Virginia Woolf?

Of course, I love old Virginia Woolf, fake that she is. I love her strange whirling rhythms. But pinned down to it, I can't think of a single thing of Virginia Woolf's that I like except her criticism. I can't think of a single novel that I like. And I've read them all. But I love her criticism and I love her diary.

What writers do you think will be remembered into the next century?

Well, that's a pretty short time. I should think quite a few. A lot of writers will be remembered for their short stories, they won't be remembered for their novels. For instance, Hemingway. A hundred years from now, Hemingway—whatever I may think of him—will be remembered, but it'll be for his short stories, not his novels. I hated *The Old Man and the Sea*. I think Faulkner would be among American writers who would be remembered for a few short stories. Maybe *Light in August*. I think Willa Cather, even though she isn't read so much today, I think there'll be a revival of interest in her work. She's an extraordinary American writer.

How about foreign writers?

Foreign writers. . . . There are a couple of South American writers that I rather admire. I like Márquez, who wrote *One Hundred Years of Solitude*. He's very talented. I don't think Camus, much as I liked him personally, will be remembered. Or Sartre or, God help us, Simone de Beauvoir.

(In the "Unspoiled Monsters" chapter of Answered Prayers, *Capote describes seeing Sartre and de Beauvoir at the Pont Royal bar in Paris: "At the time the Pont Royal had a leathery little basement bar that was the favored swill bucket of haute Bohème's fatbacks. Walleyed, pipe-sucking, pasty-hued Sartre and his spinsterish moll, de Beauvoir, were usually propped in a corner like an abandoned pair of ventriloquist's dolls.")*

Do you like Borges?

He's much too minor a writer. He's a very good writer, I like him, but he's very minor.

Were you glad to see Gabriel García Márquez get the Nobel Prize?

The Nobel Prize, to me, is a joke. They give it year after year to one absolutely nonexistent writer after another. I mean, the American writers they've given it to are beyond belief. Sinclair Lewis, Pearl Buck. It's all right that they gave it to Hemingway. It's all right that they gave it to Faulkner. But, I mean, *Saul Bellow*? And it's not just Americans. *All* of their selections are, generally speaking, very poor. It was ridiculous giving a Nobel Prize to Camus. They gave it to him on the basis of what? *The Stranger*? A couple of books of essays? I was very fond of Camus, I couldn't have liked him more, but if there was ever a minor writer, it was Camus. He edited two books of mine and I had a very interesting relationship with him, which Gore [Vidal] always resented and denied, even though the man was my editor. Gore just was not going to accept it. Why, I don't know, because Camus was not particularly his type; he only liked little dancers.

How do you assess Gore Vidal as a writer?

He's never written a novel that's readable with the exception of *Myra Breckinridge*, which you can sort of thumb your way through. It's the only book of his that's got the slightest tone of originality at all. His novels are unbelievably bad. His essays are quite good, generally speaking. Especially if he doesn't *hate* somebody too much, then they're really quite good.

Before García Márquez, William Golding got the Nobel Prize. What did you think of that?

Well! *(Laughs.)* I just thought it's one of the jokes of the century. When you think of the people who never got it—E. M. Forster, Proust, Isak Dinesen, who wanted that prize so badly—and this *nothing*... But they've been giving that prize for the last years to perfect jokes. I mean, I thought *Lord of the Flies* was one of the great rip-offs of our time. Complete steal from *A High Wind in Jamaica*. He just literally lifted the entire theme, plot, and virtually characterization from *A High Wind in Jamaica*, turned them into a bunch of small boys and placed it on an island. Otherwise it's precisely the same novel. He then wrote about seven novels, all of which I've tried to read at the time. I mean, he wasn't somebody I wasn't aware of. I never could finish them. I became completely mystified by the boredom of him. If you're going to be a literary thief, why not be a good one? And then the sudden thing of winning a Nobel Prize is such a joke. I mean, Graham Greene is a great friend of mine, virtually a lifelong friend. If they wanted to give the prize to an English writer, it certainly should have been given to Graham. I mean, this was just ludicrous, it's beyond words. Because whatever you think of Graham one way or another, Graham at least wrote one *fabulous* book called *Brighton Rock*, which knocks anything William Golding ever did, or thought of, straight through the clouds. That was one of Graham's earliest books. Fabulous book. If you've never read it, you just must read it. It's just an incredibly beautiful, *perfect* novel. It has the greatest last four paragraphs of any modern novel I can think of.

What did you think when Solzhenitsyn got the prize?

I don't really know his work and have no opinion about it. The one person who should have gotten the Nobel Prize while they were spinning it around among these... was Isak Dinesen, because she really deserved it.

You've always felt her Out of Africa *was one of the finest books of this century.*

Oh yes, because it's so perfectly written. It's so beautifully felt. Everything about it. There's not a page of that book that isn't just trembling with life like a leaf in a tree in a storm. She's a beautiful writer.

Well, Joyce didn't get it either.

They never would have given it to him. They're really a very crummy little organization, let's face it. Come on. I mean, anybody that could have given the Nobel Prize to Pearl Buck ought to go and be examined by a mental institution.

A lot of critics welcomed Saul Bellow's selection. What is it that you dislike about his work?

Oh, Saul Bellow is a nothing writer. He doesn't exist. Tell me *one* book of Saul Bellow that's in *any* way memorable, even a chapter that's memorable.

I've always liked Henderson the Rain King, *for one.*

Oh no. Dull, dull.

Have you read all of his work?

Yes, I daresay I have. I've skipped through a good deal, but I've known Saul Bellow since the very beginning of Saul Bellow and I think he's a dull man and a dull writer. Hello, Saul, how are you?

Do you feel that way about Philip Roth?

Oh, only more so. Philip Roth's quite funny in a living room but . . . forget it.

Bernard Malamud?

Unreadable.

Are there any of the so-called "Jewish" writers that you think are readable?

Norman's written some things that I like. I think Norman Mailer quite expects to get the Nobel Prize. I think that's very much in his imagination.

Who are some other possible prizewinners? How about someone like James Michener?

Well, James Michener—it's a good thing publishers have him. I'm glad he's at Random House. They're my publishers. He keeps their cash flow flowing.

Have you ever read his work?

I never have, no, so I really have no opinion. He's never written anything that would remotely interest me. Why on earth would I be interested in reading a book called *Chesapeake*?

What about someone as prolific as Joyce Carol Oates?

She's a joke monster who ought to be beheaded in a public auditorium or in Shea or in a field with hundreds of thousands *(Laughs.)* She does all the graffitti in the men's room and the women's room and in every public toilet from here to California and back, stopping in Seattle on her way! *(Laughs.)* To me, she's the most loathsome creature in America.

Have you ever met her?

I've seen her, and to *see* her is to loathe her. To read her is to absolutely vomit.

Has she ever said or written anything about you to deserve such vituperation?

Yes, she's written me a fan letter. She's written me extreme fan letters. But that's the kind of a hoax she is. I bet there's not a writer in American that's ever had their name in print that she hasn't written a fan letter to. I think she's that kind of person . . . or creature . . . or whatever. She's so . . . oooogh! *(Shudders.)*

Still, I bet she's a contender for some future Nobel Prize.

Well, Pearl Buck got it, so let 'em roll on to further triumph.

What do you think of John Updike, another possible future Nobel winner?

I'm sure he will. I hate him. Everything about him bores me. He's like a piece of mercury, you put a drop in your hand and you try to hold onto it. It's running this way and that way and you can't grab hold of it, you can't figure out what it's all about as it runs through your fingers. Anyway, he's so mannered. There's such a thing as a style, there's such a thing as a stylist. I consider myself a stylist. I consider him a mannered style, not a stylist, because it isn't even something that's his own. It's just that everything is always twisted in a certain way. You can hear how hard vocabulary is working, you become so conscious of it, so aware of it in his writing in a story that you lose, absolutely, contact with the story because of your awareness of how he's twisting a sentence, the unnaturalness of rhyme and rhythm toward this mannered thing of his which, to me, completely deadens his writing. And has from the first time I ever read his book *The Poorhouse Fair*. The moment I read that book I realized what it was, what was wrong with his writing, and my mind has never changed one little bit. He's only increased it and increased it and given it more density all the time. I told him how much I disliked his writing.

When?

You know the National Institute of Arts and Letters? We're both members and we were sitting on the stage together. They were giving out all the prizes and awards. He was talking to me and I said, "You know, John, that personally I can't stand your writing."

Did he laugh?

No, he didn't laugh at all. I said, "I don't care whether you like it or dislike it or anything, I don't like your writing. I never have. So there's no point in continuing this discussion whatsoever." I think he thought I was crazy. I was just bored with having to go on.

Let us go on to some other writers. Issac Bashevis Singer?

Don't know his work.

John Barth?

Don't know his work.

Have you ever read John Fowles?

Yes. Did you read his piece about me? He wrote a fabulous piece. It was published in the *Saturday Review* about a year and a half ago. He thinks I'm the best American writer.

Norman Mailer says that if you ask twenty major American authors who's the best, they'll all say themselves because there aren't any giants like Hemingway or Faulkner anymore, and you're all like spokes on a wheel. Would you agree with that?

No, not necessarily. I mean, Norman thinks that he's the best American writer, for sure. I think Saul Bellow thinks he is.

Let's get back to your opinion of Fowles.

I loved a book of his in which a man kidnaps a girl ...*The Collector.* I thought if he had left out the middle part of that book, and left out most of it, it would have been a real masterpiece.

Have you read anything else of his?

I read *The Magus*, but I didn't like it. I read *The French Lieutenant's Woman*, but...I think he writes very well, though.

What about someone like James Baldwin?

I got Jimmy Baldwin's first book, *Go Tell It on the Mountain*, published for him. That was just because he would never leave me alone. I was living in Paris then. He was a friend of some friends of mine. I read in the paper he had a heart attack or something. But I heard he's now a professor at the University of Michigan teaching students of advanced writing. *(Laughs, finding this very amusing.)*

What about James Jones, who was a neighbor of yours on Long Island?

Poor little James Jones. He was a sweet boy. Sweet, but not very talented. But I liked him.

Have you ever read someone like Jacqueline Susann or any of the best-selling writers like Irving Wallace or Harold Robbins?

No. All I do is make fun of them. *(Laughs.)* I caused Jacqueline Susann's death! She was lying in bed dying of cancer. I didn't know. I was on television and somebody asked me what did I think of Jacqueline Susann. And I said, "She looks like a truck driver in drag." And she was watching the show. She fell out of the bed. *(Laughs.)* Her husband picked her up. She was coughing up blood and never recovered. She sued me for a million dollars. *(Laughs.)* She was told she had better drop that lawsuit because all they had to do is bring ten truck drivers into court and put them on the witness stand and you've lost your case.

Because she *did* look like a truck driver in drag. *(Laughs.)*

I haven't asked you about any playwrights. Did you like Eugene O'Neill?

Basically, I think he was an untalented man.

Really? There are many who think he's America's greatest playwright. O'Neill, Tennessee Williams, and Arthur Miller.

Oh, well, you can check off the first and check off the last. Tennessee was good.

What about Edward Albee?

I don't know what happened to Albee.

How about modern poets? Who do you like?

That's not really my field. Among American poets I really do like Walt Whitman. I really do like Emily Dickinson. Among younger poets, I think James Merrill is very talented. I like Marianne Moore and Elizabeth Bishop. I loved Elizabeth Bishop. Until she died a few years ago, I thought she was the best American poet living.

You once called W. H. Auden a dictatorial bastard.

He *was* a dictatorial bastard. He was a tyrant.

How well did you know him?

I knew him very well, beginning in 1948. But I once had a house on an island in Italy where he had a house. I came to dislike him a lot.

Why?

He had a terrific dull rudeness about him. And he had this dreadful boyfriend. What was his name? Anyway, I remember Tennessee came to stay with me at the house in Italy and Auden and this friend of his went miles out of their way to insult him, walked past him on this tiny little beach. Because they were so jealous of his success. He was really kind of a small-time person in that way, Auden.

What do you think of his poetry?

Never meant nothin' to me.

While you were living in Italy, you got to know André Gide, who gave you a sapphire ring once. Is that true?

No. That's a story of Tennessee's. Tennessee made that story up just to make matters worse in my life. *(Laughs.)* I think he put it in his own memoirs.

Gide once said, "Do not understand me too quickly." Would you ditto that remark?

He need not have worried. *(Laughs.)* There wasn't at all a big deal there to understand. He was just a big old French queen with a rough face. *(Laughs.)* I knew him very well, you know. He had a house near me. I had a house in Sicily for two years and the last year of his life he had a house right next to me and he used to come over and sit on my balcony. I had this beautiful balcony overlooking the sea. He used to sit there all afternoon and he didn't actually quite know where he was, 'cause he was floating in and out of being gaga and then being very sensible. He'd talk very intelligently and then float back into this sort of gaga. I had to put up with him because he wouldn't let me avoid him. He was quite lonely. I wrote a long piece about him. It's in my book *The Dogs Bark.*

In that piece you say Gide wasn't very impressed with Cocteau.

Cocteau was a great friend of mine. He was a wonderful person. He was so terrifically generous. A very, very kind man. And almost too multitalented. He often said of himself it would be so much better if he could concentrate on one thing, either this, that, or the other. Gide wasn't as talented as Cocteau, by any means.

Yet, he thought he was a great deal more talented, didn't he?

Oh, Gide thought he was more talented than Proust, even though he, Gide, wrote Proust and went to visit Proust in bed. I only know this because it was all in Gide's diary.

It was fascinating. Gide, you know, was the editor at Gallimard that turned down *Remembrance of Things Past*. Proust published his book himself because nobody would publish it. And he paid for his own publication. And it was then that Gide nearly died of humiliation, because *he* had read the manuscript and rejected it. Can you imagine that old slob! He was so crusty that at his age he was chasing fifteen-year-old boys up and down the alleyways in Taormina, having them into his bedroom in the afternoon siesta hours. All the kids called him "The Five-O'Clock Menace." *(Laughs.)* He was always making dates with them at five o'clock, *à cinq heures*. I always meant to write a short story about it using his real name and everything, called "The Five-O'Clock Menace." *(Laughs.)*

Did he have any influence on you at all? Did you ever talk about writing?

No, heavens, no, no. But I used to talk to him about Oscar Wilde a good deal.

And what did he tell you about Wilde?

Oh, nothing. He didn't know too much. I just said that half as a joke. But he had known Oscar Wilde and that always rather impressed me. I had one other friend who had known Oscar Wilde. Oscar Wilde is one of the people that I would have most liked to know. I'm sure I would have liked him a lot.

What other writers would you have liked to know?

Oh, there are lots. I would have liked to know Marcel Proust.

Proust once said that great writers only create a single work.

Well, he had a reason to say that! *(Long laugh.)* He was not exactly rowing in the navy. Not even a canoe.

He also said that the plagiarism that is hardest for us to avoid is the plagiarism of ourselves.

Well, he didn't have the opportunity to do that.

How about yourself?

I've never plagiarized myself.

Another writer, Yukio Mishima, who committed hara-kiri, once predicted that you would kill yourself one day.

Mm-hmmm.

How well did he know you?

Not as well as I knew him.

How well did you know him?

I knew him very well. I don't know where he got that idea from. I must say, I never would have predicted that he would commit suicide or do what he did. I was absolutely amazed. I haven't known that many Japanese but he was one of the few Japanese that I ever met who I could talk to with a complete rapport. He had a mind that could switch onto a Western point of view just like that and I was just amazed at everything that happened to him, his killing himself that way, being beheaded, and this whole military thing. I guess I wasn't so surprised about the military thing because I knew he had sort of a semifascist mind.

Did you think he was a good writer?

Yes, I think he was an excellent writer.

What writers' reputations would be enhanced if they dropped dead tomorrow?

Practically everyone.

You mean, the best is not yet to come?

Well, it would help J. D. Salinger.

I thought he died, figuratively speaking, years ago.

Yes, well, he might as well make it legal.

Why do you suppose Salinger stopped writing?

I'm told, on very good authority, that he hasn't stopped writing at all. That he's written at least five or six short novels and that all of them have been turned down by *The New Yorker* and that he won't publish anywhere except in *The New Yorker*. And that all of them are very strange and all about Zen Buddhism.

Do you actually believe that, knowing the reputation and following that he has? That The New Yorker *would not publish at least one or two of such works?*

Yes.

I find that highly doubtful. Do you think it could happen to you? That The New Yorker *would tell you, "Sorry, Truman, we aren't interested in the next installment of* Answered Prayers"?

They would never like any installment of *Answered Prayers*.

Even if they didn't like it, do you think they wouldn't publish it?

I'm quite sure they wouldn't.

Rather elite magazine, isn't it?

But they don't like anything honest, you know. *(Laughs.)*

You've published quite a bit there.

That's neither here nor there, but you know what I mean.

All right, let's move on to writers who have run for political office, like Michener, Mailer, Vidal, and Hunter Thompson. Michener once told me he would give up all his books to have served in Congress. I would have thought the opposite: that a congressman would give up his career to have written one decent, memorable book.

Well, he hasn't, so don't worry about that. I always felt that Gore and Norman were just doing it for free publicity. They couldn't have been so foolish as to think they were going to be elected.

Mailer claims that he really believed he was *going to get elected, especially the second time he ran for mayor of New York, and was rudely shocked.*

(Laughs.) All the more so. So he thought he was going to be elected? How could he? I mean, Gore twice made a horse's ass of himself. He ran for something in New York State, then went out to California and made a bigger fool of himself. And he *really* made a fool of himself, calling up different people and asking them to give parties to raise money for his campaign.

In relation to all of the writers we've discussed, do you see yourself in competition with any of them?

I don't think of myself in terms of relationships with other writers at all and I don't feel in competition with other writers. Because I don't write about the same things as any other writer that *I* know of does. Or have the same interests. Or as a personality that's in any kind of conflict with any other writer. I have absolutely no envy of any other writer.

7

Hollywood

"It isn't even a city. It's nothing.
It's like a jumble of huts
in a jungle somewhere.
It's really completely dead."

Humphrey Bogart called him "Caposy." David O. Selznick said, "He is easy to work with, needing only to be stepped on good-naturedly, like the wonderful but bad little boy he is, when he starts to whine." Joshua Logan warned him, "Say anything you want about me, but you make fun of my picture and you'll regret it the rest of your fat midget life." John Huston loved working with him and considered him "a little bull." Marilyn Monroe told him about DiMaggio ("He can hit home runs. If that's all it takes, we'd still be married.")

During the filming of *Murder by Death*, Capote got up from his seat by a table where he had been impatiently waiting for the next scene to begin. As he paced, a six-hundred-pound wrought-iron chandelier came crashing down from the ceiling, crushing the table. Without a beat, Capote cracked, "Gore's got to be somewhere in the wings."

In his book of travel pieces, *Local Color*, he wrote of Hollywood: "But how very correct, after all, that here at continent's end we should find only a dumping ground for all that is most exploitedly American: oil pumps pounding like the heartbeat of demons, avenues of used-car lots, supermarkets, motels, the gee dad I never knew a Chevrolet gee dad gee mom gee whiz wham of publicity, the biggest, broadest, best, sprawled and helplessly etherized by immaculate sunshine and sound of sea and unearthly sweetness of flowers blooming in December."

In spite of his declared hatred of the place, he seemed drawn to it, returning often. Joanne Carson, who called him "my protector and my best friend," furnished a room in her Bel-Air home just for him.

Once, producer and showman Alan Carr, who made so much money with *Grease* he could spend the rest of his life throwing lavish parties, threw a black-tie dinner for Capote in an abandoned jail in downtown L.A. Guests like Lucille Ball, David Niven, and Rod Stewart, who had no idea what they were getting into, were fingerprinted and had "mug" shots taken.

"He had given that spectacular black-and-white masked ball," Carr said, "so I wanted to give him something to match that, but in a different way. It wasn't more spectacular, but it was probably more inventive, since we had to take an abandoned jail that all the cop shows use as a set and refurbish it. The flowers, champagne, and food all had to be brought in. Truman loved it."

If he found Hollywood to be "the surface of the moon" in disguise, "the noplace of everywhere," Capote also recognized that "Old people love California; they close their eyes, and the wind through the winter flowers says sleep, the sea says sleep: it is a preview of heaven."

Why do you so dislike Los Angeles?

Ha! Let's not get into it.

Does it have anything to do with the time you were subpoenaed by a California court and you escaped to New York but were eventually jailed back in California?

Oh heavens, no. Good Lord, that was funny. I wrote it all in *Music for Chameleons*. They wanted me to testify against a boy who had already been convicted and was going to get a retrial. In between, he had given me an interview. The understanding was I would never publish any of it and never tell anybody what he had told me. Well, he told me *every*thing and he had never told anyone else everything, including his lawyer. Somehow, they knew that I knew. They tricked me, coming to my house ostensibly to talk about something else and served me with a subpoena. If I had acknowledged it, it meant that I had to testify against this boy, which meant that in my profession, people could not trust to tell me something without... you know. So I had to bite the bullet. So I left California during the trial and stayed out of California for a year. He was reconvicted anyway, which I knew he would be because they had all the evidence they needed, that's why it made it all so ridiculous. I came back because I was going to do the Manson trial for *The New York Times*, but I was arrested for insulting the court and the judge gave me an indeterminate sentence. I was in jail and my lawyer that I had in California hadn't bothered to study the subpoena. My lawyer from New York came out there and took one look at it and said, "This was all illegal because they have arrested you as a citizen of California and you're a citizen of New York." They had to let me go like that. *(Snaps fingers.)* But I was in jail for a day.

They also fined you, didn't they?

Five hundred dollars. And didn't return it, either.

So this obviously didn't enhance your feelings toward California.

I've always disliked California.

And especially Hollywood, which you've called evil. Why?

(Laughs.) I just despise it. I like the title of Alison Lurie's book, *The Nowhere City*. I think she's one of the five best young American writers. It isn't even a city. It's nothing. It's like a jumble of huts in a jungle somewhere. I don't understand how you can live there. It's really, completely dead. Walk along the street, there's nothing moving. I've lived in small Spanish fishing villages which were literally sunny all day long every day of the week, but they weren't as boring as Los Angeles. There just doesn't seem to be a reason to do anything and nothing *to* do when you get up. Or if there is, it's too hard to do it, everything is seventy miles away. How ghastly to wake up in the night to smoke cigarettes and you don't have any in the house.

What's happening with Handcarved Coffins, *which producer Lester Persky paid a half-million dollars for and which has gone from one studio to another?*

The script was written three times. I didn't write it.

The same girl, whose name I have a marvelous, wonderful capacity to not remember, either her first or last name, did three scripts, all of which were turned down by me. They were terrible. I said, if you don't get rid of this girl, I'm going to take my book back. And I don't have to give them back a penny. One director, Jonathan Demme, whom I liked, said he was ready to go ahead with the last script after he finished a movie he was making, but that amazed me because I wasn't. So someone new was brought in.

Was that Sidney Lumet?

Yes. Sidney can be very good.

Is the script done yet to your satisfaction?

No. It's being redone.

The story ended where Quinn, the suspected murderer, doesn't get caught. Doesn't that create a problem for the film? Will it end the way you wrote it?

That's the whole point. If it doesn't end that way, they're idiots. That *is* the ending. And they're just trying to wreck it. I don't know. Lester varies. Some days I think he understands it and other days I think I made a very bad mistake.

Was Quinn the killer?

Of course he's the killer.

When you met him, did he know who you were?

Sure.

And he's now living where?

Right there.

"Right there" is never identified in the story. Do you think anything will ever happen to him?

No. He was never accused of anything. That's why I had to be so careful in the book. If ever I was going to have a lawsuit, that's where I was going to have a lawsuit. And I wasn't going to have a lawsuit.

It's a bizarre story, where various townspeople receive small replicas of a coffin with their photos inside and then are gruesomely murdered by ingenious methods—a razor-sharp steel wire hung between two trees beheads one victim, another is poisoned with liquid nicotine, another is attacked in his car by rattlesnakes injected with amphetamines. Did you invent any of that?

That's *exactly* what happened. That's one of my best pieces of reportage.

Why did you choose to write the story in almost a play or interview form?

That was something I'd been doing for a long time. I wanted to move with great rapidity. I wanted it to move with fantastic speed. I didn't want to fall into an *In Cold Blood* form. I wanted it to move as fast as the rattlesnake bites. And technically, that was the method that I felt moved fastest.

Do you think the movie will ever get done?

I don't know. I think they're planning to start it soon, but you never know.

Who would you like to see play Mr. Quinn?

Carroll O'Connor. And he wants to play Quinn. He's an extremely good actor. Very, very, very good.

Hasn't there been some talk of a remake of Breakfast at Tiffany's *with Jodie Foster as Holly?*

Yes. I was a great fan of Jodie Foster before anybody ever heard of her. I saw her by accident. She made a lot of movies in France, she speaks French. And I have a house in Switzerland, in a little village, and I saw movies there that were never shown in America. That's the first time I ever saw her. I saw her in a fabulous musical [*Bugsy Malone*] where she sang a song called "My Name Is Tallulah." All the characters were children playing grown-up gangsters. I thought it was charming. Most of my friends hated it, but I loved it. Then she did a film called *The Little Girl Who Lives Down the Lane*. The movie wasn't good, but she was.

When did you get to know her?

I don't really know her at all. Except through this talk of a remake of *Breakfast at Tiffany's* with her as Holly Golightly. But that's not why I think she's very talented.

Do you think she was affected much by John Hinckley's obsession with her?

People have had far more shocking things happen to them. Think about that girl who had been kidnapped, buried alive, tortured for four days. It just happens I met her and talked to her and she's turned out to be an absolutely wonderful girl, very attractive and not particularly neurotic.

Was she very religious?

(Deep voice) She was just Southern. *(Laughs.)*

Back to the movies, would you like to see a remake of Breakfast at Tiffany's?

Yes, because the other one wasn't correct.

What was wrong with it?

Oh, God, just everything. It was the most miscast film I've ever seen. It made me want to throw up. Like Mickey Rooney playing this Japanese photographer. Well, indeed I *had* a Japanese photographer in the book, but he certainly wasn't *Mickey Rooney*. And although I'm very fond of Audrey Hepburn, she's an extremely good friend of mine, I was shocked and terribly annoyed when she was cast in that part. It was high treachery on the part of the producers. They didn't do a single thing they promised. I had *lots* of offers for that book, from practically everybody, and I sold it to this group at Paramount because they promised things, they made a list of everything, and they didn't keep a single one. The day I signed the contract they turned around and did exactly the reverse. They got a *lousy* director like Blake Edwards, who I could spit on! They got George Axelrod to do the script. I will say that they offered it to me, but I don't like to do scripts of my own work, I prefer doing scripts of other people's.

Would you consider doing the rewrite of Breakfast *though?*

I would pick the person and work closely with him, so that we don't have any misunderstanding of who this girl Holly is. She is *not* a chic or lean bone-faced Audrey Hepburn; she's a smart girl, but smart in an entirely different way.

More like Jodie Foster?

She's ideal for the part.

When you were young, were there any movies which left some kind of impression on you?

It's hard to say. I remember the first movie when I was more or less a child. It made a great impression on me. It was *Of Human Bondage*, of all things. I can't say exactly why, but it's the first movie I remember making a real impression on me.

Didn't you write the screenplay of Henry James's The Turn of the Screw?

Yes, it was called *The Innocents*. I had loved *The Turn of the Screw*. I read it when I was a child, thirteen. When it was offered to me to do it as a film, I said yes instantly, without rereading it. I was in Germany at the time, doing a series of lectures at the university in Munich, and I thought, if they had gone to all the trouble to track me down to this ghastly place, it must mean something. So I said yes right way. Then I let several weeks go by before I reread it and then I got the shock of my life. Because Henry James had pulled a fantastic trick in this book: it doesn't stand up anywhere. It has no plot! He's just pretending this and this and that. It was like the little Dutch boy with his finger trying to keep the water from flooding out—I kept building up more plot, more characters, more scenes. In the entire book there were only two scenes performable.

I had that experience again when I did *The Great Gatsby*. Again, I did the same thing when it was offered to me. This was the most recent version—my script was not the one finally used, thank God. I mean, the picture was a no-terms no-terms about it. Although I wrote it. It was a fascinating script to work on because what I had to do when I reread the book and studied it... it was like a strange mystery—it was Henry James all over again. There were only two scenes in the whole book that were filmable.

Which two?

One is when they go to the Plaza Hotel and get sort of drunk; the other is when the mechanic goes to the house to shoot him, it actually has a narrative movement. But everything else is a flashback or a flashforward. That's fine in prose, but it's not in the movies. You cannot keep flashing forward and back continuously.

Did your appreciation of those works increase or decrease once you began taking them apart?

Decreased immensely.

Maybe great novels don't make great movies.

Very rarely. *Wuthering Heights*—it wasn't a great movie but at least it had the atmosphere of the book. It was a great book.

Psycho *was a better movie than it was a book.*

I read the book out of curiosity, after seeing the movie. Basically, I didn't think either one of them was good. The movie was obviously much better than the book, but still, Hitchcock left too many gaps. He took advantage of the viewer. To me, it was never really explained why the boy in the motel had this psychotic feeling about his mother and how, in fact, she got stuffed and put into that chair. It's a rather smelly business. And he kept sinking all those things into that tiny little swamp—it would take all of Macy's to hold that stuff. *(Laughs.)*

The best acted piece in that film, the one who really saved that movie, was—

Anthony Perkins?

No, I can't stand him. I don't think there's anything to him. No, it was the guy who played the detective. I used him once and he won an Emmy—I did an original television play called *Among the Paths to Eden*. I forget his name [Martin Balsam.] He's a wonderful actor, he's been in hundreds of movies, but he's never been the star.

What did you think of John Huston's Moby Dick?

I didn't like it. I also didn't like *Moby Dick* the first time I read it, but then I was about thirteen. The second time I read it I was about thirty and somewhere along the line I liked it a great deal. My old friend John . . . he hated Montgomery Clift. And he hated Marilyn Monroe. But if you ask him, he'll just say (*imitating Huston's deep voice*): "Oh, I just love Marilyn, I put her in her first picture and in her last." Clift was originally set to do *Reflections in a Golden Eye*, you know, but he was uninsurable. So Elizabeth Taylor guaranteed the insurance, but then Clift died and Brando agreed to do it. I always found that curious. Marlon was totally wrong for that part.

What did you think of Huston's adaptation of Flannery O'Connor's Wise Blood?

He butchered the novel, which is my least favorite Flannery O'Connor novel. I didn't like the movie very much.

His last major book to film was your old friend Lowry's Under the Volcano.

It's very nice that John is still working so well at his age.

Do you think he knew Lowry?

No, he didn't know Lowry. I knew Lowry before I knew John.

Are you interested in seeing his film?

Sure I'd like to see it, because of John, because of Malcolm, because of the book. I don't really particularly see it as a film. Who wrote the screenplay?

A young writer named Guy Gallo. Huston may have had a hand in it.

Oh, John has never really written a screenplay.

Well, his name is certainly on a lot of major films as screenwriter. He's credited with The African Queen, The Treasure of the Sierra Madre...

Yes, well, he's also credited with me for *Beat the Devil*, but he never wrote a word of *Beat the Devil.* I think he wrote one thing: the screenplay for *The Maltese Falcon.* And I think he wrote before he ever directed, he wrote several screenplays because he had to. But after that he had other people.... He was like Irving Berlin, who has the little nigger boy in the trunk (*laughs*) who writes all the songs.

Aren't you really being unfair to Huston? Surely some of Beat the Devil *was in collaboration?*

It was *all* mine. I wrote every day it was being made. I was always just one day ahead, sometimes I was down there in the morning distributing the script to the cameramen and the poor actors. But I must say, everybody enjoyed it thoroughly, the whole experience. Except me, because I was up all night and was exhausted. It was totally mad, but it was meant to be. It was a big success finally, but at first it wasn't. It has a sort of cult following.

How well did you get to know John Huston?

I knew him and know him extremely well. I lived in the same room with him. Everybody thought we were having an affair, including Humphrey Bogart, who lived next door to us, and he spread it everywhere—the sounds that he could hear in the room at night between me and Huston, Huston had finally gone that way, etc. And Huston played straight into it, because he thought it was very funny. Half of the crew were scarcely speaking to him, they were so appalled. *(Loud laughter.)* It was a very funny situation. I enjoyed it, I thought it was quite funny, I didn't mind it a bit.

Did it last that way throughout the making of the entire movie?

Oh yes.

But in reality, while you were writing during the night, what was he doing?

When I was working he was sleeping. Actually, he was playing cards and drinking.

Do you play cards at all?

No, I don't like cards. I did as a child, I was a very good cardplayer. I was very good at bridge in boarding school. When I was thirteen I suddenly stopped playing cards and never have since. I can do it in a minute if you suddenly said: We desperately need a fourth.

(In May 1984 I spent a week in Puerto Vallarta, Mexico, traveling each day by car and boat out to John Huston's home at Las Caletas. I was interviewing Huston for an upcoming issue of Playboy *magazine. Naturally, I brought up Capote. Huston*

was plainly enamored of the man. "He's an extraordinary little man who has the courage and the determination of a lion," Huston told me. When I brought up Capote's assertion that he alone wrote Beat the Devil *while Huston spent his nights playing poker, Huston looked at me with that wizened, sagacious face of his and said, "We wrote together." The subject, as far as he was concerned, was closed.)*

What was your impression of Humphrey Bogart?

Humphrey Bogart was a wonderful person. We were very good friends right up until when he died. Bogart had a wonderful kind of chip on his shoulder, you know. He was very charming, very kind to me always. I liked him a lot.

Is that rare among actors—to like them?

No. I liked quite a few. I can't think of any actors I particularly dislike.

How close were you to Montgomery Clift?

Oh, he was a great friend of mine. He caused me a lot of trouble. He was sort of running wild the last few years of his life. He used to come over to visit me and invariably he broke something, accidentally. I lived through all of that period of Monty Clift's life with him. He was just impossible. He came to my apartment in New York one night and set fire to the whole kitchen. He was so completely batty. I had to have five fire trucks come to put out the flames. But he was a very gifted, talented, intelligent person. Very sad story. Confused.

I knew him from the beginning to the end. I knew him when he was a very young actor working for the Lunts. I knew him before he ever made his first movie.

Was he aware of his talent?

Oh, yes.

Why do people who have talent like that seem to be so self-destructive?

I don't know, because Monty wasn't really like that until he went into the movies. He was a relatively happy person. Fabulously talented. Then, after he made *Red River*, he suddenly started to become quite destructive. He didn't really want anybody to know about his life or to know what kind of a person he really was. And that carried beyond the normal thing of people not wanting to reveal too much about their private lives. He got it developed inside his head, something to do with his career.

It's a peculiar profession to be in and expect that nobody would pry into your private life.

Well, so many of those boys, like Tony Perkins, who, virtually at the same time, was going through the same problem of nobody knowing whether he was really gay, et cetera. The difference with Monty was that Monty was having these affairs in which he was terribly emotionally involved. *(Laughs.)* I think that was the whole key to his problems.

That he just couldn't face up to his sexuality?

Oh, he could face up to *that*.

He just couldn't face up to others knowing about it?

He couldn't face up to . . . like, for instance, I love that lousy little Kevin McCarthy. In the two books about Monty they have things about Kevin McCarthy and what a great friend he was to Monty. And in the books, Kevin McCarthy says he had no *idea* that Monty Clift was homosexual and was absolutely *amazed* when a producer said to him that he had best watch his relationship with Monty Clift for his own career, et cetera. Why, he said, it never crossed his mind. Well, it had crossed the mind of every single trolley-car conductor in Hollywood, so it was very difficult to believe it hadn't crossed the mind of his best friend for going on seven and a half years. *(Laughs.)* I mean, how far can hypocrisy go?

Clift always reminded me a lot of Marilyn Monroe. Marilyn always said, "The only person I know who's worse off in life than me is Monty Clift." It's funny, 'cause they more or less had the same problem.

You've written two pieces about Marilyn; one was published in The Dogs Bark, *the other in* Music for Chameleons. *In the first, you open with: "Monroe? Just a slob, really..." Was she?*

Oh, no. That's what *she* thought I thought of her. No, I loved Marilyn. I thought she was wonderful. Now, there's someone whose death shocked me. I was in Spain in a little town and I saw it in a Spanish newspaper. I could really scarcely believe it. Although, I don't know, she tried to kill herself at least four or five times to my certain knowledge during the years I knew her and I'd known her ever since the first film she ever made—well, the first film that she ever had a speaking role in, *The Asphalt Jungle.* John Huston directed it and I met her through him.

Have you ever written about her previous suicide attempts?

No. I wrote that portrait of her in *Music for Chameleons* but I didn't go into that.

Is that portrait, "A Beautiful Child," your favorite one of a personality?

No, in that book my favorite one is called "A Day's Work," the portrait of the woman that cleans houses.

Why do you suppose Norman Mailer is so fascinated with Monroe?

'Cause he didn't know her.

Did Marilyn actually say, "I like to dance naked in front of mirrors and watch my titties jump around"?

Yes.

Did she know that you might one day write about her?

I didn't know that I would, either. All of that comes out of my journal. That entire piece came out of my journal.

You end that piece asking, "Why does life have to be so fucking rotten?" Is that the way you feel about life in general?

I meant it in terms of her life... and I meant it about certain points of my own, yes. Generally speaking, I don't think about it that way. It was a question I was asking Marilyn, who appears sort of like as a ghost at the end of that piece. There you were speaking to a ghost.

Marilyn told you of Errol Flynn playing the piano with his penis. Is that a common Flynn story?

I just don't know whether it is or not.

Did it surprise or shock you that she liked to talk about this kind of thing?

I told you, I'd known her a long, long time. Nothing about Marilyn could ever surprise me.

Except her death.

Yes, that surprised me.

You've written about your own affair with Errol Flynn when you were nineteen....

Well, that was scarcely an affair. You can call it an evening together.

What kind of man was Flynn?

He was nice. He had a lot of manners. He read a lot and he was more intelligent than people thought.

He also had a wild-man reputation.

I didn't know him that well. Altogether I only saw him maybe three times in my life.

Did John Gielgud ever teach you how to rhumba?

John Gielgud never taught me anything. He's an old

friend of mine but he never taught me how to rhumba. *(Laughs.)*

That's in Brinnin's essay about you. He has you saying to him, "I was out until three a.m. with Mr. John Gielgud. He taught me how to do the rhumba."

I guess I must have skipped some parts of that.

He also tells of your meeting with John Garfield. What was your impression of him?

Oh, he was a very fine, very kind person. Very sweet and very intelligent. I liked him very much.

And Charlie Chaplin, whom you also knew?

I knew him ever since I was seventeen years old, because his wife, Oona, is exactly my age and we were sort of childhood friends. So, as soon as she married Charlie, I used to go and visit them all the time. My house in Switzerland is only about a half-hour from their house, so I used to go over there all the time.

What was your opinion of Chaplin?

I loved Charlie, he was a wonderful man.

Marlon Brando said he was mean and sadistic, the kind of man who was either at your feet or at your throat.

Well that movie [*The Countess from Hong Kong*] was such a disaster and Charlie was so unhappy, he knew he was not doing a good job and that his time had gone past. I wouldn't have wanted to work for him, I can see that.

Apparently Brando didn't want to either.

Well, he should never have taken that part. He read the script. He must have seen it was very bad.

Did you also know James Dean?

Yes, I knew him. I didn't think very much of him. I knew him when he was in New York, he was a good friend of several friends of mine. And he did that Gide play. I don't think he was very good in the play, to put it mildly.

What about his movies?

I never thought anything about him as an actor. I didn't think he had any quality at all.

Brando did.

Well, Brando told me that Jimmy Dean used to call him on the phone all the time and Marlon would listen in on the phone and listen to him talking to the answering service, you know, and he wouldn't answer, wouldn't speak up. This was one of the more disgusting aspects of Marlon's. *(Laughs.)*

Brando told me he tried to get Dean to see a psychiatrist.

Marlon was just getting frightened, that's all. *(Laughs.)*

Did he have to be frightened more about Dean or about Montgomery Clift?

Oh, well, you see, Marlon realized that Monty was really talented! Monty was a real threat to Marlon. Had Monty lived, he would have overcome Marlon, I think.

When Last Tango in Paris *came out, some critics thought it was the most erotic and liberating film ever made. One critic went so far as to say it altered the face of an art form. What did you think about it?*

I think it's a terrifically bad movie.

And Brando's performance?

Considering the fact that he had nothing to work with, he did quite a remarkable job. I think the scene where he has his soliloquy with the dead wife, with this absolutely nonsensical writing that's in the movie all the way through, he did an incredible job, because he actually made you believe in this character and his relationship with the dead wife and this peculiar grief. He did quite an extraordinary job of working with absolutely nothing.

When I asked him what the film was about, Brando answered

it was about Bertolucci's psychoanalysis, and then said he really had no idea what it was about.

Mm-hmmm. *I* have no idea what the movie was about, either.

Do you think, though, that it broke new ground sexually for the movies?

It was certainly vulgar beyond words. That dialogue was, to me, quite offensive.

Have movies often offended you?

No, but I found that movie quite offensive.

Norman Mailer is a great fan of Last Tango. *He's written an essay about it.*

Well, I said he thinks William Burroughs is a genius.

Why do you suppose Brando displays such a disdain for his profession?

All male actors have a disdain for their profession. Women actors have a totally different feeling than men do about their profession. All the men I've ever known, professional actors, have a slight feeling that they're doing something that isn't exactly what they ought to be doing. They feel some slight guilt about it. It's sort of as though what they were doing wasn't masculine or somehow has some effect on them of making them rather, seemingly, bisexual by nature. Do you follow what I'm trying to say? The only actors I've ever known that don't feel that way have all been gay. I mean people of the highest talent and the greatest quality. In fact, the best actors we had, they don't have that feeling. Practically the entire English theater is made up of nothing but extraordinary, gifted, gay male actors.

How close were you with Noël Coward?

He was a great friend. Not a lover, but a very great friend. I couldn't have been more fond of anybody. I used to go to stay with him a lot in Jamaica. He was always kind to me right from when I was a child, comparatively speaking.

And Fred Astaire?

Love him. He's delightful, charming, a great artist. Far more original and superior artist to Nureyev and Baryshnikov.

Baryshnikov once said if he could dance like anybody it would be Astaire.

Well, he's more original. He's a great original artist.

Isn't he also a strange man?

He is quite strange. I knew him through Jock Whitney, who was a best friend of one of his best friends. If I had known him through somebody else maybe I would have gotten a different impression about him. Fred so loved Jock Whitney that with Jock he always was at his absolute Astaire best. That's the way I saw him.

In the column you wrote for Esquire, *you described Garbo's apartment. When were you there?*

Many times.

You observed she had no mirrors—was that true about the bathrooms and her bedroom as well?

I never was in her bedroom, that's why I said in the public rooms. I was in the bathroom, but that's not a public room.

Do you know if she was bothered by what you wrote?

She wouldn't be bothered or annoyed. She's quite a good friend.

Would she laugh at your description of her paintings being hung upside down?

I think so, because I told her several times that she should have this investigated. She has about four Picassos, and two of them, I'm absolutely certain, are upside down.

There's still a great fascination with Garbo.

All I know is everybody that I know is always fascinated by her. I have a friend who saw her on the street a week ago and practically passed out. He followed her for blocks. She doesn't know many people, but she's outgoing if she trusts you. She's got a terrific sense of humor and a marvelous laugh. She's a frightened person. But you have to know her very well to discover that. I knew her for years before I realized how frightened she was.

But her public behavior, or nonbehavior rather, would indicate that she was frightened.

I know, but I mean *really* frightened. I've known her at least thirty years and in those years she's let at least three or four people take fantastic advantage of her. They discovered this fear in her and worked on it. One of them had her scared out of her wits. For some reason, he liked me or I would never have been friends with her, because he wouldn't let her be friends with anybody. She's now living with the Baroness de Rothschild's sister, they've been living together for about five, six years. And she's terrifically nice to Greta. She has a house in Paris where she lives most of the time. She's in New York now.

Garbo is probably the woman most editors and publishers would like to get to, because she's never talked. She and Jacqueline Onassis.

Well, Jackie better not go on a talk show. She wouldn't know what to say. *(Does a crude imitation of Jackie):* "What did you say? Oh, Johnny, did you really mean that? That I'm a whooore? You didn't really ssssay that, did you, Joooohny?" I can do a really good imitation of her, given the right material. I hate her. I used to be great friends with her. I hate her. I absolutely despise her.

Let's hold off talking about her for the moment and finish with your thoughts on movie stars. Did you ever know Robert Mitchum?

No, but I admire him. I think he's an extremely good actor and very, very consistent in his career. He's never been given the credit he deserves. Did you ever see a movie called *Night of the Hunter*? He was marvelous. That was a fabulous movie. Charles Laughton directed that. Didn't you think it was good? So well-directed.

What about Rod Steiger?

Oh, Rod Steiger's the worst actor that ever lived. The very name makes me throw up.

He's made some good pictures.

Oh, he's so terrible. He's one of the world's worst hams. A real *jambon*!

How about Elizabeth Taylor?

I like Elizabeth. I think she's a good actress, too. Given a little bit of something to do and a good director, she's all right. I don't understand what happened to *Private Lives*. I didn't see it, but it's hard to believe that it could be that bad, or that she could be that bad, because it's an easy play.

What do you think of Shelley Winters as an actress and a writer? She was a friend of Adlai Stevenson's, too, wasn't she?

Mm-hmm, very good. Her book was rather interesting. She sort of bores me as a person.

And what about some of our more contemporary actresses, like Diane Keaton, Meryl Streep, and Jane Fonda?

I like Diane Keaton. Meryl Streep, I think, is the Creep.

Why is that?

Ooh, god, she looks like a chicken. She's got a nose like a chicken and a mouth like a chicken. She's totally untalented as far as I'm concerned. Jane Fonda has always been, to me, a fake and a bore.

A fake in what way?

Just a fake. I've known her since she was a child. I remember going to her house in New York when she was about sixteen years old. I was sitting having a conversation with her father and she threw a fit on the living-room floor, rolling and crying about some dress she wanted to buy that he wouldn't let her buy. He was a very stingy man, I'll admit, but I mean, ucch, she's a throw-up number.

You don't think she's had a genuine change of values?

She's had a genuine change of bank accounts. I think it's nice of her to support her husband in his ridiculous political activity.

What's your opinion of Robert DeNiro?

I can never recognize him from one movie to the next, so I never know who he is. To me he's just an invisible man. He doesn't exist. There's this person the screen says is Robert DeNiro and then on comes somebody you never saw before in your life.

But does that person hold your attention?

No, he's never given a performance that held my attention at all.

He's often touted as Brando's successor.

Well, perhaps he is. Who knows? I don't know anybody that I think is any better than he is. It isn't that I'm saying. It's just that I don't ever recognize him on the screen.

What about Al Pacino? Have you ever seen him on the stage in American Buffalo*?*

I hate that play. Can't stand it.

Elliott Gould once told me he sat next to you on an airplane and you had a terrific conversation.

Yes, I liked him, we had a good time. He was very nice.

Do you know Woody Allen?

Very talented, but very uneven. He can do things that are quite surprising, then he can be a complete stiff. I certainly wouldn't go out of my way to see a Woody Allen movie.

Let's talk about you as an actor. Have you ever been stagestruck?

I've never been the least bit stagestruck.

How did appearing in the film Murder by Death *affect you?*

Having written so many film scripts, it was interesting to be on the other side of the camera. I thought it was going to be fun, sort of a lark. It was a vacation for me. But it turned out to be anything but a vacation. I hated it. It was incredibly boring. All the waiting and the waiting and then I didn't like the script. At first I thought I would like it. I mean, Neil Simon wrote it for me.

How do you assess your performance?

I thought I was fine, for what it was. The only person who didn't like me was John Simon, which I ought to take great honors about. I didn't get any bad reviews except from that wretched man with a German accent.

What about the movie of your life, when it's made?

That will not be made. *(Laughs.)*

You never know. You once joked that Greta Garbo should play you.

Yes, Greta would love to do it, but...

You've got someone else in mind?

Well...

Who?

The ghost of Eisenhower.

8

Jackie O, Gore Vidal, and Joseph Who?

"There are people I would erase out of my life with a blowtorch."

When a publication called *Fag Rag* asked Gore Vidal if Capote would be very rich when he died, Vidal responded, "Capote has no money." *Fag Rag*: "Really? Living at UN Plaza?" Vidal: "This is one of the reasons why he has no money. He thinks he's Bunny Mellon. . . . He thinks he's a very rich Society Lady, and spends a great deal of money."

Vidal went on to call Capote "a Republican housewife from Kansas with all the prejudices."

When Monique Van Vooren asked Vidal in 1976 if he had seen Capote lately, he answered: "I've seen him about once in twenty years and I had an impression that the one time was probably too often. It was at Dru Heinz's.

I didn't have my glasses on and I sat down on what I thought was a poof and it was Capote."

In *Tennessee Williams' Letters to Donald Windham*, Williams asked Windham in March 1949, "Tell me! What do you think Truman is, a bitch or not? I can never quite make up my mind about it."

The playwright had a falling-out with Capote in Naples when Capote did an imitation of an actress saying that *Summer and Smoke* was "the work of a dying writer." "I was almost hysterical with hurt feelings and rage at Truman," Williams wrote. "The next day I got over it, the rage... and Truman was all sweetness and light, we embraced, and there was at least an apparent reconciliation but that mischievous tongue of hers remained fairly active the whole time we were there [in Ischia]. I think you judge Truman a bit too charitably when you call him a child: he is more like a sweetly vicious old lady."

JACKIE O, GORE VIDAL, AND JOSEPH WHO?

If you could live your life over again, knowing what you know, would you like to change many things?

I would like to erase some things with the biggest rubber eraser going. Some things I'd leave in print or in picture form or whatever, and some things I would erase completely.

Things that you have written?

No, no, nothing about my work. In my life. There are people I would erase out of my life with a blowtorch.

Would one of those people be Gore Vidal, whom you dislike?

Oh, dislike is scarcely the word.

Your relationship with Gore has always seemed strange…

My whole life with Gore has always been so strange, except in the beginning, when we were very friendly.

In Brinnin's essay, he describes a scene when you were in North Africa and Gore Vidal came to your door on a Sunday morning, all "hopped-up and crazy-eyed" saying, "Truman, they're out to get us," and acting very paranoid. Is that true?

Yes. I have no idea what happened. All I know is that Gore and I were sort of friends when were were teenagers. Sort of like at MGM, Judy Garland and Lana Turner were friends as teenagers. We were friends among the literati when we were teenagers. And suddenly, one day, I had lunch with Gore and Tennessee and I said something and nobody can remember what it is I said. I don't remember. Tennessee couldn't remember. Apparently, Gore can't remember. Whatever it is that I said, he flew into a complete rage. I've never seen anybody so angry and from that day onward, it was a feud that he fueled, not me, because I never paid any attention to it and I never knew what started it and I never knew what it was about. And I still don't.

And from that misunderstanding comes so much enmity?

Well, wouldn't you dislike somebody who sued you for a million dollars? He's now cost me, in legal fees, over eighty thousand dollars, which I've actually paid. If somebody sues you, you have to get a lawyer and defend the case and it all costs a lot of money. Gore had no more reason to sue me than you do, other than he's just paranoid and goes off the deep end.

So, if you were at a party and Vidal appeared, would you walk out?

No. I don't pay any attention to Gore. It means, to me, absolutely nothing. As a matter of fact, I'm not even basically angry with him about all of this. To me, it's just crazy, that's all.

You'd like to call quits to the feud?

I have never pursued the feud. I have never done anything to agitate it. I am totally innocent in this whole thing. It's just Gore. Gore has an obsession about me. Much as I don't really care about psychoanalysis, I think he ought to go to an analyst and find out what it is that's bothering him so much.

Do you think he might be jealous, in any way, of your work?

Of course he's jealous. Gore has never written anything that anybody will remember . . . talk about fifty years from today, they won't remember it ten years from its last paperback edition. See, Gore has literally never written a masterpiece. Now, even J. D. Salinger has written a masterpiece of a kind. Flannery O'Connor wrote a masterpiece or two. Hemingway did. Faulkner did. Scott Fitzgerald did. Norman never has. We could go on and on, but he has not done the one essential thing: he has not written an unforgettable book or a book that was the turning point in either his or anybody else's life. Without that, it doesn't matter how much he does or what he does because he'll be just like Joseph Hegesheimer. Do *you* remember Joseph Hegesheimer? Fifty years ago, Joseph Hegesheimer was five thousand times more famous than Gore Vidal ever thought of being and today, right at this moment, you don't even know who Joseph Hegesheimer is. All I can tell you about him is he wrote a book called *Three Pennies. Three Black Pennies.*

Then Vidal ranks high on your dislike list?

No, no, he's not worthy of it.

You've named some of the names on that list in Music for Chameleons*—people like Billy Graham, Princess Margaret, Princess Anne, Ralph Nader, Byron White, Werner Erhard, Madame Gandhi, Masters and Johnson, Sammy Davis Jr., Jerry Brown... Who's at the very top of that list?*

Well, let's see. Mrs. Onassis, or whatever she's calling herself these days. Her sister, the perennial Princess Lee Radziwill. Richard Nixon....

Why Mrs. Onassis?

Because she's insincere. She's a person who basically has nothing but contempt for most everything in the world.

Is she an unhappy woman as well?

An opportunist like Jackie, who's making out on her opportunism most of the time, isn't exactly unhappy. I'd say she's never been happy because she had a great disappointment in her childhood and she's been trying to make up for it ever since. So I wouldn't use that word, it doesn't mean anything. But she's a very opportunistic, insincere, vain, rather mean person.

Do you know anything about her relationship with Jack Kennedy?

Well, she once said to me, "If I had to describe Jack, I'd describe somebody with a very tiny body and a huge head." That was said with a certain displeasure. This was before he was elected President. I've known her a long time. I've known her before she was married.

It certainly sounds like something has happened to turn you so against her.

Just insight. And experience.

About Kennedy—you once described a dinner party you attended where Senator Jack Kennedy listened enraptured to someone talking about Las Vegas showgirls.

Yes.

Could you recall that scene?

Yes, I remember it exactly. I can see the room, I can see the people. It was in a very small apartment on Park Avenue. The ladies had left the table after dinner and the men were supposed to be having their brandy and cigars and this person was just giving a description of all the high-priced whores in Las Vegas that he had tried out that they would enjoy. He had their telephone numbers with what they did—how well they sucked cock, how much, how long, how big a one they could take, and did they take a trip around the world, everything they did, how big their tits were. Everyone was very interested in tits. Oh, it was just disgusting, absolutely a stomach-turner. And the future President—he wasn't the President then—was doing everything but jotting notes down in his notebook. He *was* jotting something on a napkin. But this person used to pimp for him all the time. He was the one who used to get all of these high-priced call girls which Kennedy had *much*, much, much more than the public had any idea of. He had a real bad case of satyriasis.

And how did Jackie deal with that?

She just put up with it. He didn't do it right in front of her face. He sort of managed to get rid of her over weekends and whatnot. That's why he bought that house in Virginia. She would be sitting in the house in Virginia and the wife of a foreign industrialist, with whom he was having this great affair, would fly in to give him a blow-job in Washington.

Does anybody know about that?

I know about it. Certain people do.

All right, let's get back to Jackie once and for all and get to the root of your anger. What actually happened to make you feel the way you now do about her?

Well, it started with her sister. I'm not really going to go into this because it's just too long and too involved. Her sister was a great friend of mine. I had been very nice to her sister. Now, Jackie and Lee have always despised Gore. I mean, the things they said to me about Gore... and when Gore brought that lawsuit against me about what I said in some stupid interview that I was talked into doing by Dotson Rader, because Dotson Rader had this friend who wanted to be a writer, and Dotson, who wasn't especially a friend of mine, or even a friend, kept calling me relentlessly that this magazine, whichever one, would give him an assignment if he could get an interview with me, and Dotson, in effect, kept saying, "Oh, please, please, if you'd do this..." Well, you get the picture. So finally I said, Oh, for Christ's sake, it can't make that much difference—though it did make a tremendous amount of difference, as it turned out. Anyway, this interview appeared, which was absolutely ridiculous. I was asked did I know why Gore Vidal had turned against the Kennedys so much? I said: Of course, everybody knows that. Which everybody did know . . . all of which George Plimpton and Arthur Schlesinger have written about. So I repeated the story in this interview, and Gore, in his mad hysteria and hatred of me, promptly sued me for a million dollars. Lee was the person who had told me the story. So my lawyers asked her for an affidavit and her lawyer told her not to give anything and, in fact, to give one to Gore's lawyer saying she never told me anything of the kind. And he was also Gore's lawyer. And Jackie backed Lee up in this by total silence. And at that moment I just realized what a hypocrite and what a deeply insincere person Jackie was. I was *terribly* hurt. I could not understand Jackie, because we had been friends for much too long. So the next time I saw Jackie I cut her absolutely dead. It was at a small dinner party. I walked in and saw that she was there and I said—and I was perfectly sober—I said to the hostess, "Why didn't you tell me this tramp was going to come so I wouldn't have come." And turned around and walked out. Now, maybe you can say that's a horrible, cruel, vulgar thing to do, and it certainly shocked that room half out of its wits . . . but I don't regret it for one minute.

Did you ever attempt to talk to Jackie about this matter directly?

No. She knew what was going on.

Maybe she just didn't want to embarrass her husband.

I don't care. This man was suing me for a million dollars about something that had actually happened and which she and her sister had both told, leaving me in a situation which has now cost me over eighty thousand dollars in just legal fees. That's not funny.

What I don't understand is, if Schlesinger and Plimpton have both written about it, as you say...

They've all given me affidavits.

So how could the suit continue?

Because it's been to court twice and both times the judges turned it back, saying send it to a higher court. I will win, but I'll never get a nickel back.

Have you thought of countersuing?

I'm not going to countersue because it would cost me a lot of money and...who cares? I don't give a damn one way or the other. I think Gore bitterly regrets having got into this.

He can't just drop it?

He's sent all kinds of messages. Yes, he would like to get out of it. He said he would get out of it if I would pay his lawyers. Then he said he isn't asking me to pay his lawyers, what he's asking me to do is to write him a letter of apology for having said what I said and admitting that it wasn't true. And my opinion is that I have nothing to apologize about and what I said was true, so I'm not going to write any such letter. So he can just continue his suit into eternity. I'll just take it down the line till he drops it by the wayside. One or the other of us is sure to go, whether in the next bubonic plague...

This has certainly become quite a literary feud that will be talked about in years to come.

Magazines have devoted whole issues to it.

So you see yourself as a victim in this affair?

It's all been extremely unfair to me. I'm sorry about the whole thing. I'm sorry that Jackie and I came to a falling-out to that degree on such a subject, such a level, about something I had nothing to do with, basically. Lee is the real villain in this little drama.

You've had noted battles with well-known people and a lot of it has been because you've named names, said what's on your mind. Do you ever regret any of that?

I can't remember any of my battles that I regret. In fact, I would relish a few more. *(Laughs.)*

(Not very long after this conversation, Truman agreed to issue the following legal settlement letter which the newspapers subsequently printed:

> *Dear Gore,*
>
> *I apologize for any distress, inconvenience, or expense which may have been caused you. . . . I was not present at the event about which I am quoted in that interview, and I understand from your representatives that what I am reported as saying does not accurately set forth what occurred.*
>
> *I can assure you that the article was not an accurate transcription of what I said, especially with regard to any remarks which might cause aspersions upon your character or behavior, and that I will avoid discussing the subject in the future.*
>
> *Best,*
> *Truman Capote*

I asked Truman about this over the phone but he didn't want to talk about it anymore. "It's over with," he said, "there's nothing more to say about it."

That was one battle, I felt, that he may or may not have regretted, but that he certainly didn't relish.)

9

Impressions

"There was a necrophiliac bar
in the Village and I went there once.
It was a place of just people
who liked to go to bed with dead people."

"Quite a lot of people disliked him," observed Saint Subber, who produced Capote's *House of Flowers* and *A Grass Harp* on Broadway. "I knew him over forty years. To me, he was a Roman candle. He was always celebrating life."

Wrote John Fowles, "We European innocents think of Truman Capote mainly as a writer. I know he is seen otherwise in America."

Not exactly. Andy Warhol, for one: "I admire people who do well with words," the artist recorded in his *Philosophy*, "and I thought Truman Capote filled up space with words so well that when I first got to New York I began writing short fan letters to him and calling him on the phone every day until his mother told me to quit it."

Pati Hill, who wrote her impressions in *The Paris Review*, felt, "His approach to anyone new is one of open curiosity and friendliness. He might be taken in by anything and, in fact, seems only too ready to be. There is something about him, though, that makes you feel that for all his willingness, it would be hard to pull any wool over his eyes and maybe it is better not to try."

John Malcolm Brinnin's first impression of the young Capote, at an artists' colony called Yaddo in upstate New York, was that "He looked like no other adult male I'd ever seen. His head was big and handsome, and his butterscotch hair was cut in bangs. Willowy and delicate above the waist, he was, below, as strong and chunky as a Shetland pony. He wore a white T-shirt, khaki shorts too big for him, sandals that fit as neatly as hooves.... His voice, odd and high, was full of funny resonances that ran a scale of their own: meadowlark trills and, when he laughed or growled, a tugboat basso."

Harold Robbins has teased, "He'd be all right if he took his finger out of his mouth." And Tennessee Williams joked, "I always said Little Truman had a voice so high it could only be detected by a bat!"

Proust once said that the impression is to the writer what experimentation is to the scientist. Are you in the mood to experiment with some impressions?

Go ahead.

Let's start with Andy Warhol.

Andy is a very shy person with an extraordinary talent to get other people to do things for him. In that factory he runs down there, he has thirty-five or forty people, more or less unpaid, who are doing all these incredible things for Andy and one can't exactly figure out what the grip is. It's sort of like a strange orphanage for would-be talented people.

Do you consider him an important artist?

Well, he's had a great influence over an enormous number of people. When he was a child, Andy Warhol had this obsession about me and used to write me from Pittsburgh, when he was a high-school student. When he came to New York, he used to stand outside my house, just stand out there all day waiting for me to come out. He wanted to become a friend of mine, wanted to speak to me, to talk to me. He nearly drove me crazy. But I've had many obsessive people like that.

Such as?

There was a secretary at Random House who had this obsession about me which was absolutely unbelievable. Sent flowers every day. She became so obsessive and so dreadful that I asked Random House to do something about it. She used to come and stand in front of my house. I have one at the moment, a fairly new one, about a year now. At least he's not in this area. He's in Texas. But he writes me every single day.

Have you ever acknowledged him?

No.

You're not very fond of two of this country's major artists, Jasper Johns and Robert Rauschenberg, are you?

You call them artists? I wouldn't pay twenty-five cents for a painting by either Rauschenberg or Jasper Johns. Especially Jasper Johns. I have a Rauschenberg, but somebody gave it to me. It's in a closet. Hello there, Bob!

Are there any living artists you like?

That takes considerable thought. I like a lot of artists but none of them are living that I can think of. There must be some living artist I like.... Well, I like Francis Bacon.

What about David Hockney?

Oh, well, as a sort of joke. I kind of like him. I really wouldn't care to have anything of his. Every now and then I see something of Hockney's in somebody else's house that looks right where it is.

What about Henry Moore?

No, I dislike his sculptures. They bore me.

I once asked Moore to compare himself with Picasso, but he was only interested in putting himself where he felt he belonged, among Rembrandt and Michelangelo.

You mean he, himself?

Well, he wasn't talking about Duchamp.

I couldn't care less about Duchamp. If he got run over

in the street right in front of us, I'd go outside and wouldn't bother to help them pick up the bones.

Wasn't it Colette who turned you into a collector of French paperweights?

Mm-hmmm. She was a wonderful writer, too.

And do you travel with these paperweights wherever you go?

Oh, yes. I like to have them, they give me a feeling of ... if I wake up in a motel room and look at a table and see them, it's something familiar. I don't collect them anymore because they're too expensive. But I have a fabulous collection.

Let me ask you about some designers. Halston?

Very talented young man.

Calvin Klein?

Very talented young man. *(Laughs.)*

All right, let's move on to entertainers. Didn't you know Elvis Presley?

Elvis Presley gave me the only dinner party I've ever heard of his giving, in Las Vegas. I had a house in Palm Springs and he had a house there—he and his manager, Colonel Parker. So I used to see Elvis occasionally. He lived very near me and he was going to open at this big hotel in Las Vegas. He was making sort of a comeback. He hadn't appeared in public in a long time and he invited me to come up to see it, 'cause I had never seen him. In fact, I really had never heard any of his records, either. So he said if I would come up, he would give this dinner party for me. I was more curious as to who in the world would he invite to this dinner party than I was about anything else, so I went with a friend. The one and only time I've ever been to Las Vegas.

We saw the opening show and the dinner party was in between shows. I can't say that I was at all impressed by his performance. So we went down to this apartment he had there in the hotel and the dinner party consisted of about eight young men and *one* old friend of mine who had flown all the way from Honolulu to come, mainly because she was a fan of Elvis'. She loved Elvis, and guess who it was? Doris Duke. *(Laughs.)* So we had this dinner party. This table was full of orchids up and down and everything looked very fancy in a gauche, peculiar way. But the dinner was incredible. It was all kinds of different things, fried pork and fried chicken and fried catfish.

Did Elvis ever read your work?

I don't think so. I doubt it. He was nice, I sort of liked him.

You also knew John Lennon, didn't you?

Oh, I liked John Lennon. I knew him a little bit and I liked him a lot. He was very intelligent. He was a sensitive, very good-hearted person. I couldn't stand her. The Jap. She was always paranoid. The most unpleasant person that ever was, in my opinion. She's a bore.

Do you think she hurt his creativity?

I think when the Beatles broke up they all hurt each other irrevocably. I don't think any one of them amounted to a hill of beans since then. You watch what happens to the Rolling Stones. Mick Jagger will never do anything. Keith Richards is absolutely batty. The others are competent, but they're pretty old and far gone. I went on that tour with them and you could see that whole thing beginning to fall apart.

Are you surprised they're still together?

No, I suspected then that they'd be together for about another ten years. Keith Richards is the most talented person in that group.

That tour you went on with them, weren't you commissioned by Rolling Stone *magazine to write about it?*

That's not really true, I wasn't commissioned to write anything. The Rolling Stones were on this tour and Mick Jagger asked me if I'd like to go along for a while. I did know Jann Wenner, and *Rolling Stone*... mmmm, I can't remember if they'd just done a long interview with me or if they did it a little bit later, but anyway, he had said something to me about writing a thing, but I had no intention of writing anything about the Rolling Stones' trip. I was curious about going for a while and I did go for two weeks. But at the end of the two weeks, I had had enough of the Rolling Stones. I never wanted to hear another Rolling Stones record or anything connected with them.

Why not?

I just found them all kind of quite mad. I mean, there was this airplane and you'd get on it right after they'd finished the concert and they were all looped immediately on every conceivable kind of... There was this drink that they all drank called a tequila sunrise. And this girl, who was supposed to be a stewardess, would pass down the aisle with this plate full of every kind of pill you can imagine. And you're supposed to take the pills and drink the tequila sunrise. Then, up at the front of the plane, there was this very well-known man who made documentary films who was making pornographic movies of different people with the Rolling Stones company, including the Rolling Stones, having sex with some total stranger that they had picked up in the town we'd just been in. It was like being in a blue movie for two solid weeks.

Would you call that decadence?

No, I don't know what decadence means, really. People use it in such varied ways. This was their way of doing whatever they were doing and they weren't really causing any harm to anybody.

What is your opinion of Mick Jagger?

Mick is a bore. I thought they were all boring. I never cared about the Rolling Stones as performers. If you've seen Mick perform as often as I did, you come to have absolutely no feeling about him as a performer at all, except isn't it extraordinary that he has that much energy and is able to reproduce and do the same thing over and over again with such precision. I mean, there's no variation *whatsoever* in their concerts. Everything is precisely the same. Every beat, every lyric, every movement. And there's something about the total lack of improvisation, where they're pretending to be improvising and spontaneous all the time, which is wearing. But I think he's an extraordinarily keen, sharp businessman. The moment he walks off that stage he pulls a computer out of his pocket. He's about as square as you can possibly be.

The guy who plays the saxophone with them, Bobby, he's very talented, but out there. Then there's the other one who plays the piano, he's very square. Oh my God, is he square. It always amused me how he came to work, all dressed like he was a Brooks salesman in the hat department. Then he'd go into his trailer and put on his Rolling Stones drag and come out and get ready to go onstage. He'd play the piano in this wild, frenzied way and then the program would end, the balloons would come down, and he'd march like a little tin soldier to his trailer, put on his Brooks Brothers clothes, and walk out with the crowd. *(Laughs.)*

Are there any rock groups that you like?

I can't think of any as a group, offhand, no. I've liked certain songs, certain records.

What about the songs of Bob Dylan?

I've never liked him, I've always thought he was a fraud. He's certainly not this simple-minded little boy with these little, simple lyrics, etc. He's another opportunist with a very sharp career-minded knowing-where-he's-going. He's also insincere. Just look at the wonderful turn his whole career has taken, back from those songs of the sixties to what he does now. He's right up there with Baby Snooks at the moment. I never did understand why people liked Bob Dylan. He couldn't sing.

I think a lot of us felt that he put into words what the sixties were about—more than most writers did.

Well, it obviously didn't mean very much to him.

We've talked earlier about two singers you really liked, Billie Holiday and Lee Wiley. What about another mood singer, Morgana King?

Morgana King has just one little trick, letting her voice get higher and higher and higher till it just simply disappears somewhere, and she does every song the same way. There's just this one little style. When I first heard her, I was amused by it. But in a short time, there's nothing there.

If you have time to go see a show, go see *My One and Only*, a musical. It's very charming. It's so delicately put together, it's absolutely delightful. It's got two people in it that I like. There's a colored tap dancer about sixty years old called Honi, who is absolutely fabulous. And I love Twiggy. I've always liked Twiggy. And it's got a great score. I want to see Jerome Robbins' new ballet, *Glass Pieces*.

How about books—are you reading much lately?

There are a couple of books I want to read. I read mostly old books.

Fiction or nonfiction?

Half and half.

And television? Do you watch things like "The Tonight Show"? Wasn't Johnny Carson once a neighbor of yours in New York?

Oh yes, for years. I felt extremely sorry for his wife. I feel even sorrier for her now. Not this new wife, she's divorcing him. But his second wife, Joanne. She was very good to him. She did a tremendous amount for Johnny. I don't think Johnny would have survived or have had remotely the career he's had if it hadn't been for her. But he was *mean* as hell to her. And they lived right next door. He would holler and get terribly angry and she would take refuge in my apartment. She would hide and Johnny would come pounding on my door, shouting, "I know she's there." And I would just maintain a dead silence.

Did you ever talk to him about this?

I knew Johnny pretty well, but nobody knows Johnny. He has no friends. Just the people of his staff there. Well, he has more friends now than he used to when I knew him. When I knew him, he really had no friends at all. I don't think even now he has friends, he just knows more people. The only time he comes alive, you know, is on camera. The moment the camera goes, so does he. But I have nothing against Johnny Carson.

You also have nothing againt Billy and Rosalynn Carter, isn't that true?

I think Billy Carter's the nicest person in his family. He was always completely honest. And Mrs. Carter certainly surprised me because I knew her a little bit before he ran for office and she struck me as a very intelligent person, extremely well-read.

Why haven't you ever voted?

Never been living anywhere long enough.

Certainly you've lived in New York long enough.

Now I am. I mean, I'm never anywhere longer than three or four months.

Do you think people should vote—or doesn't it matter?

Oh, I think they should. I think everybody should get out and vote against the Catholics. *(Laughs.)*

What politician do you find interesting? You're on record for liking Ronald Reagan before he became President.

I've always liked him.

Why?

He's a much more intelligent person than people seem to vaguely understand. And he makes me laugh a lot.

What's your opinion of Castro?

Castro's an interesting person. I'd like to know him better. I think he has a rather good mind, basically sympathetic. He's had a terribly bad press.

What about the leaders of the Soviet Union, who keep on changing. Have any of them interested you?

I thought Andropov was an intelligent, cool man who certainly ran his department extremely well in Russia. Considering the amount of time I've spent in Russia, he never appeared on my horizon at all. And I knew everybody in Russia. That's what I mean by very smooth, very quiet profile. I'd heard of him but I had no idea he was that influential. I *thought* I knew everybody in Russia.

Do you think there's an increase in tension between Russia and the U.S.?

No. Just more posturing. I think there's a great deal

more to that Korean airplane story than any of us know.

Or will know?

I suppose we will know. But they were in there for two hours, they were photographing. Because that particular thing is one of the biggest Soviet secret bases there is. Do you know that under an ice floe there they have nineteen submarines with nuclear missiles in that particular place that they were flying over?

Let's move from spying to perversity. I read something once about a necrophiliac bar in the Village that you used to go to. Is there any truth to that story?

Oh, that's a story. There *was* a necrophiliac bar in the Village and I went there once. I was taken there by . . . Who was it? It was a place of just people who liked to go to bed with dead people and they had a bar where they met and exchanged addresses of funeral parlors. *(Laughs.)*

So there weren't actually corpses available at the bar?

Oh no, no, no. It was like Twilight. Do you know that bar in New York called Twilight? *Well,* it's not in the telephone book. It's on the East Side in the Twenties. It's fascinating. It's really one of the most fascinating bars that I've ever been to. It's a bar where young boys and men meet. Very attractive young, beautiful boys who have obsessions about older men, anybody over sixty. And that's the thing they're interested in sexually. These elderly gentlemen go there and these unbelievably attractive boys, young executive types, come in there to vie with each other to pick up the old. It's strange, but, in a way, it's not depressing. You should go there once. Everybody seems to be enjoying themselves. There's a certain kind of pleasantness about the atmosphere. Of course, everybody knows about how obsessive certain young people are about much older men. They aren't looking for fathers, they're looking for grandfathers.

Where did you find out about it?

From a friend of mine who likes older men. Beautiful young man, extremely. And he told me about it and took me down there.

Since we're on such topics, could you recount the recipe you once described at a bordello in New Orleans, the Countess Willie Piazza's cherry dessert?

Well, you take whipped cream, you heat cherries, fresh cherries, boil them, and take this thick cream—this is after you've warmed up the cunt with hot-water bags. After you've got everything warmed up, then you stuff the cunt up with red cherries until she's fully packed and then you pour this cream into the whole thing and then the guy eats it out, cherry by cherry.

Did you just hear about this?

Oh no, it was famous.

Did you know the Countess?

No, she was a bit before my time.

Is there anyone we haven't mentioned that I should be asking you about? Why do you so dislike Billy Graham?

I just think he's a complete, total phony. I'd like to see *his* Swiss bank account.

Why do you imagine so many people are attracted to him?

Oh, because they're all so stupid. *(Laughs.)*

You certainly sound like you have a tragic view of life.

Who doesn't in their right mind?

So, who's left?

Well, there's a *total* creep, whom I'll call Mr. Bidet, who's the First Lady's First-Lady-in-Waiting. He's Mrs. Ronald Reagan's First-Lady-in-Waiting. He's a creep who crawls around New York from party to party, who took up the Reagans about ten years ago. He's sort of rich, inherited a certain amount of money, and spends all of his time being what's called a "walker." A "walker" is a man who has absolutely nothing to do in his life except get up in the morning and have lunch with a rich woman and then walk her all afternoon from one store to another. Mr. Bidet is high on my list.

Sounds that way.

He's in *Answered Prayers* as a character. In the book, he's called Mr. Bidet, because he has a face shaped exactly like a bidet.

10

Answered Prayers

> "*Answered Prayers* would kill my last
> chances of ever winning anything...
> except, perhaps, twenty years in jail."

In 1959, Norman Mailer made a prophetic comment about Capote. "I would suspect he hesitates between the attractions of Society, which enjoys and so repays him for his unique gifts, and the novel he could write of the gossip column's real life, a major work, but it would banish him forever from his favorite world. Since I have nothing to lose, I hope Truman fries a few of the fancier fish."

Answered Prayers was the frying pan Mailer had hoped for. It was to be Capote's masterwork—a nonfiction novel culled from his diaries, letters, and journals written between 1943 and 1965.

"All the characters were real," Capote wrote in his preface to *Music for Chameleons*. "I hadn't invented anything. And yet *Answered Prayers* is not intended as any ordinary roman à clef, a form where facts are disguised as fiction. My intentions are the reverse: to remove disguises, not manufacture them."

He described the book as "a thriller" about the journey of "a frustrated, not very moral, but extremely sensitive and intelligent person, down through the interior of the earth; there, the central character, P. B. Jones, finds spoiled and unspoiled monsters."

(In one of the published chapters, P. B. Jones acknowledges: "I knew I was a bastard but forgave myself because, after all, I was a *born* bastard—a talented one whose sole obligation was to his talent.")

Capote's lawyer, Alan Schwartz, said the book "was not entirely autobiographical, but it did deal with a character that was a kind of male Holly Golightly."

Capote liked to talk about the book—perhaps too much. He told *People* magazine, "I'm constructing it in four parts, and actually, it's like constructing a gun. There's the handle, the trigger, the barrel and, finally, the bullet. And when that bullet is fired from the gun, it's going to come out with a speed and power like you've never seen—*wham!*"

The parts that did come out—"Mojave," "La Côte Basque, 1965," "Unspoiled Monsters," "Kate McCloud"—in 1975 and 1976, had that power. Enough power, in fact, that it paralyzed Capote and sent him whirling into a dark depression and a nervous breakdown. His high-society "friends" were suddenly slapped awake with the realization that a writer among them—especially one as sharp and perceptive as Capote—was dangerous. Doors he had spent a lifetime prying open were now beginning to close on him.

He told Clarke Taylor in the *Los Angeles Times*, "There's a real misconception about the book, which is not about the rich or celebrated, although I can't blame anyone, having the chapters published out of context."

Arnold Gingrich, the editor-in-chief of *Esquire*, which published the four installments of *Answered Prayers*, came to Capote's defense. "Much of Proust, it must be remembered, is gossip, and most of Boswell, but both stand as better portraits of their eras than whole stacks of tedious tomes devoted to exhaustive analyses of the underlying characteristics and tendencies of their epochs."

"He always said this would be the last book he would ever write," said his friend Joanne Carson. "It was by far his most difficult. He was letting his barriers down in this book and writing from his heart and soul."

Gore Vidal, on the other hand, never believed the book existed. He told Judy Halfpenny in 1979: "Mr. Capote never wrote *Answered Prayers*. It is the Madonna of the Future all over again. But as this is America, if you publicize a nonexistent work enough, it becomes positively palpable. It would be nice if he were to get the Nobel on the strength of *Answered Prayers*, which he, indeed, never wrote. There were a few jagged pieces of what might have been a gossip-novel published in *Esquire*. The rest is silence; and litigation and . . . noise on TV."

John Fowles had higher hopes. In a 1980 *Saturday Review* book review of *Music for Chameleons* he wrote: "I take it *Music for Chameleons* is a foretaste of what we can expect when *Answered Prayers* is finally rewritten and published, and I now look forward to it immensely. So, also, I suspect, somewhere under a café awning on Parnassus, do Mr. Capote's three masters: Flaubert, Maupassant, and Marcel Proust. . . . If I'm not quite sure yet that he will one day join them there, I think he begins, behind the froth and the brouhaha, the name-dropping and the back-stabbing, the wicked penchant for recording how real people spoke and behaved, to make a serious bid for their company. And of one thing I am certain: Contemporary literature would be much, much duller and poorer without him."

Is Answered Prayers *the book you hope will really rattle teeth?*

When I'm writing something, I truly cannot think about what anybody's reaction to it is. That's why I made a great mistake by publishing any chapters of the book before. I should have just published the book, wham! by itself. That was a big mistake publishing those four or five chapters because they were very misleading as to what the book is really all about. But I never think about what anybody's going to think about anything because, otherwise, I would just freeze up.

James Michener said you would be remembered well into the twenty-first century if you ever finished Answered Prayers. *Do you feel that expectations have been too high regarding your book?*

No. I mean, I don't think about it. I truly don't. I never think about it. I have a way of blocking things completely out of my mind and I have had since I was a child, because I've had a lot of things to block out of my mind. Things that create anxiety and apprehension and whatnot. And I just can. It's just as though I took some kind of magical pill or something, but I just drop it completely out of my mind.

Do you feel that Answered Prayers *will be the book you will be most remembered by?*

Yes, I suppose so.

Even more than In Cold Blood?

Well, I hope to write other books after this. I have another book in mind which I think is extremely good. In fact, I'd love to be working on it now.

Do you have the ending to that other book already done?

Oh yes, I've had the ending for years. I haven't written a word of it, I've only worked it out in my mind.

Are the last chapters of Answered Prayers *written?*

Yes.

Will they change?

No, it won't change. It inevitably has to end this way. It's one of the few novels I know that has a genuinely happy ending. *(Laughs.)* You'll close with a smile and a tear... after having gone through an awful lot of pain and torture.

You started writing it back in 1972. Over the last dozen years, how much time have you spent on it?

About four years.

Why has it taken you so long to finish it?

The reason it's taken so long is because I keep changing it, the structure of it. And because I stop working on it for long periods of time and write something else. And then I come back to it with a lot fresher feeling. It's a book of a great deal of density and intensity. You can only work on it for a certain length of time without becoming quite a nervous wreck.

Isn't it difficult, though, to go away from it for such long periods of time and keep coming back to it?

It's great for me to go away from it for periods because it improves it. You get a better, longer view of what it is that I'm doing. That book's been improved so much by the fact that I actually didn't work on it at all for over a year.

It became so much clearer and sharper and shrewder and severer and self-critical. Out come the scissors. *(Laughs.)* I'm all for the scissors. I believe more in the scissors than I do in the pencil.

So, when are we going to finally read this book?

That's a secret between me and God. And bein' a Southern boy *(goes into a thick Southern accent)*... I believe in what Jesus tells me... and when Jesus tells me, "Hand that over"... or the bank tells me, "Hand that over..." *(Laughs.)*

Where do you feel most comfortable working on the book—here in Sagaponack or in the city?

Depends. If I make up my mind and just turn off all the telephones, I can sometimes do better in the city than out here.

Christopher Isherwood once said that before he publishes anything he always sends a copy of his manuscript to the people he's writing about. Have you ever done that?

I showed a lot of people who were in *Answered Prayers* the chapters of it that they were in, yes.

Did any of them say you went too far?

No. It's very strange. Nobody really complained about it until after it was published.

Have you had any pangs of guilt from anything you've written or published so far?

No.

No worry about lawsuits?

I don't expect to have any lawsuits. I mean, I may get one out of left field, which I seem to receive, like with

Breakfast at Tiffany's. I was sued by a girl whom I never met, saw, or heard of who claimed she was Holly Golightly. That's happened to me, with great injustice, three times now. But if I'm sued, it will be a phony.

When have you last written a section of Answered Prayers?

I recently finished a long section which leads up to the end just a few weeks ago.

So, perhaps we won't have to wait too much longer?

I don't want to think about it or discuss it. I'm *tired* of that subject.

Well, at least it's nice to know that you have a sense of the whole book now.

We'll have to wait and see. I really mean that, because I don't know myself till I see what the whole thing's about. I know basically what's in my head and what I'm doing, but I don't know really what the end result will sound or feel like.

You dedicated your last book, Music for Chameleons, *to Tennessee Williams. What does a dedication mean to you?*

It's a gesture of friendship.

And who will you be dedicating Answered Prayers *to?*

I haven't decided. I may not dedicate it to anybody.

I know you've ridiculed the Nobel Prize, but do you think, once this book is published, that you might receive it?

No, no. I'm the last person in the world. And especially *Answered Prayers* would kill my last chances in the world of ever winning anything. Except, perhaps, twenty years in jail. *(Laughs.)*

You're one of the few writers in our country who have penetrated the upper crust of our society. Louis Auchincloss also writes about the rich. What do you think of his work?

I think he's a second-rate Stephen Birmingham. And Stephen Birmingham is third-rate. *(Laughs.)*

Besides yourself, are there any writers who have written with insight about the rich?

No, because they don't know anything about the rich. Actually, if Gore could write, which he can't, it's just possible Gore could write something of the rich, that world. But I'm not so sure, because Gore hasn't really lived too much inside that life since he was a child and I don't know that Gore really knows too much about it.

What do you consider rich?

In this day and age, you've got to have *at least* five hundred million dollars. Free. That you can pick up. I know somebody who has a yearly income just from one thing of five million dollars that he doesn't have to pay *one* penny of tax on. Not one cent. And every time I look at him it makes me furious. He's a very generous man who's given millions to museums, to colleges, to try to buy his way out of this thing. He inherited the money, he never made a dime of it. But I guess something about his getting that five million dollars a year and never having to pay a penny tax on it makes me want to throttle him.

You yourself made something like three million dollars from In Cold Blood, *didn't you?*

I made more than that.

And did the government take half of it?

They took a great deal more than half of it. I pay very high taxes.

And resent it all the way.

Every step. But I've never in my life been in a situation—and this is something you can believe or not believe—I don't even know exactly why, considering how expensive my life has been, but I've never needed to do anything because of money. If I'm going to do something though, I want to be paid for it, let's put it that way.

You don't use an agent, either, do you?

No, I like to sell my own things. Except for movies, because those contracts can get too complicated. I always have a pretty good idea of what to get. I do get the most, I think, of practically any writer in America, as far as what I am paid for something. I just got twenty thousand dollars for a four-thousand-word piece from a magazine.

Which magazine?

That's for me to know.

Malcolm Brinnin noted that by the time you were in your early thirties, you had gone through a number of stages: from old friends to show-business acquaintances to international society. Did you always have Answered Prayers *in mind as you became, what Brinnin calls, a mascot for café society?*

Well, I was never that. I had a lot of rich friends. I still have a lot of rich friends. I don't particularly like rich people. In fact, I have a kind of contempt for most of them. I'd say most rich people I know would really be totally lost more than any other kind of person I can think of if they didn't have their money. That's why money means so much to them, why they're so desperate and fixated on the subject and why they hang together so closely like a bunch of bees in a beehive, because all they really have is their money. If they didn't have it, they would just be without absolutely anything.

So the answer to the question "Are the rich different?" is "Yes, they have more money"?

No, no. The real difference between rich people and regular people is that the rich people serve such marvelous vegetables. Delicious little tiny vegetables. Little fresh-born things, scarcely out of the earth. Little baby corn, little baby peas, little lambs that have been *ripped* out of their mothers' wombs. That's the real difference. All of their vegetables and their meats are so incredibly fresh and unborn.

11

Drugs, Booze, Depression, and Death

"I don't care about the past.
I want to know about tomorrow."

In November 1977 Capote lasted just five minutes onstage at Towson State University in Maryland before university officials removed him. They said he was drunk and was mumbling obscenities.

In July 1978 he appeared on the Stanley Siegel show claiming he hadn't slept in two days and began to ramble incoherently about his mixing alcohol and medication. Among the drugs he took were Valium and Librium. He liked to drink vodka and occasionally daiquiris. "I put them together like some sort of cocktail," he told Siegel and his New York television audience. Siegel soon became uncomfortable and, losing control of the interview, he stopped it after seventeen minutes. One TV critic wrote, "A talented man of considerable literary stature was making a fool of himself in front of 250,000. But strangely enough, it was drama."

His descent into his own private hell brought him to a rehabilitation center for the "chemically addicted." He stayed a month at New York's Smithers Institute, three months at the Hazelden Foundation in Minnesota.

"I knew my problems and I really had no choice," he said. "I had to learn to handle my anxieties without the aid of chemicals—or else."

He began to feel that his writing was "becoming too dense" and "began to have doubts." So he attempted to simplify, reconstructing "in a severe, minimal manner, commonplace conversations."

One of these he had with his alter ego, what he called his Siamese twin. He challenged his belief in God and came to the conclusion that "life, plain living, took away the memories of whatever faith still lingered. I'm not the worst person that's crossed my path, not by a considerable distance, but I've committed some serious sins, deliberate cruelty among them; and it didn't bother me one whit, I never gave it a thought. Until I had to. When the rain started to fall, it was a hard black rain, and it just kept on falling. So I started to think about God again."

But the "hard black rain" kept falling. In August 1981 he collapsed from a convulsive seizure in the lobby of the UN Plaza, where he lived. In April 1983 he had another seizure and was hospitalized in Montgomery, Alabama. Tests showed a "toxic level" of Dilantin and phenobarbital—the drugs he used to control his epilepsy—in his system.

A few months later, in Sagaponack, he was arrested for driving under the influence and without a license.

The last years, like his early years, were difficult, depressing, dark. Talking to his Siamese twin, at the end of "Nocturnal Turnings," he tries to get some sleep.

"But first let's say a prayer," he tells himself. "The one we used to say when we were real little and slept in the same bed with Sook and Queenie [his dog], with the quilts piled on top of us because the house was so big and cold....

"Now I lay me down to sleep, I pray the Lord my soul to keep. And if I should die before I wake, I pray the Lord my soul to take. Amen."

And then he bids himself good night. "I love you," he says. "I love you, too," he answers.

"You'd better," he says. "Because when you get right down to it, all we've got is each other. Alone. To the grave. And that's the tragedy, isn't it?"

"You forget," he answers. "We have God, too."

In Other Voices, Other Rooms, *Dolores says to Joel that it's strange how long it takes us to discover ourselves. How long has it taken you?*

I think I discovered myself very early on, it's just taken me a long time to discover how much endurance I have for pain. How much pain I can actually withstand and still function.

How much pain are you in?

I don't know. How much pain is anybody in?

Well, how have you been feeling lately?

I had this terrific attack of pleurisy, which is something that's a mystery. They don't really know what it is.

What are the symptoms?

Oh, the symptoms! *(Laughs.)* The symptoms are upon you like Dracula! You suddenly can hardly breathe . . . and with every breath you take, each one is a knife stabbing you right through your chest. It's absolutely ghastly. It's very difficult to find any position to lie down or sit down or stand up or anything. You can't really stand up. You're completely hunched over by the pain. It's ghastly.

Is the pain located in one area?

All through here. Right across your chest. If you didn't know what it was—and I only know because I had an attack of it two years ago for the first time and the doctor knew instantly what it was—you would think you were dying of a very severe, strange heart attack. It's all in your chest. You break out into a sweat. But if you know what it it is, it's nothing.

What can be done about it?

You rest. There's really no known medication for it and it doesn't react to antibiotics. Antibiotics don't seem to affect it at all. There's a kind of a strong-tasting syrup drink that after a while the pain stops, every three, four hours. Otherwise, you would just die of sheer pain by itself. The thing is to knock you out as much as possible into a kind of a coma or sleep.

Is it at all like an anxiety attack?

I've had an anxiety attack. It's different. An anxiety attack is physical but it's also mental. About fifty-fifty, when you believe that something dreadful is going to happen any minute, like you're on the drop of the gallows. Having watched so many people on the drop of the gallows, I know how that feels, having held their hands at the last moment. Sometimes, when I have these anxieties, I think about people like Perry and Dick, having lived through their lives to their deaths. I identify with them completely, remember how they felt up until the very last minute, thinking: My God, I have some nerve to be annoyed or upset or anything, thinking about what they went through.

But I always seem to have something wrong with me. I always have a cold or bronchitis or something. I was convinced that I had an ulcer but I had a CAT scan and they said I don't.

Weren't you once operated on for cancer in the 1960's?

Mm-hmmm.

That must have been a very bad time.

No, it wasn't very. Well, there was a certain concern about it. It was rather painful. It's funny, it's gone out of my mind. I've really scarcely ever thought about it from the time it happened.

Weren't you hospitalized in Alabama not long ago because of an epileptic seizure?

Yes. I flew to Birmingham to visit my aunt. The plane was late and they were going to drive the seventy miles to pick me up, but as it turned out, I never made it to see her. I have this thing I have to take called Dilantin. If I don't take it, I have a kind of epilepsy. What happens is I have a sort of seizure and I don't feel it coming on. As long as it lasts, I don't feel it at all and I don't know what is happening to me. When I come out of it, I'm usually in a hospital.

Are you catatonic when it happens?

No, apparently I move a great deal. I have never had a really good description given to me by anybody of what it is that I do. The pills will stop you from having them but you have to be sure to take them. I have forgot for two or three days and nothing's happened, but it's very dangerous, you're taking an awful chance.

But when it happens, it usually alarms people enough to send you to a hospital?

Yes. The last time, I didn't come out of it for two days in the hospital.

Is it usually a few days before you come out of it?

I don't know. I don't know nothing. I only know what people tell me.

What do people tell you?

Apparently, the one person who's seen me through a lot of this, Jack Dunphy, says I do a great deal of talking.

Are you talking coherently?

No. See, I really truly don't know. It's not a rare thing.

Is this what Dostoyevsky had, where he would fall down and foam at the mouth?

I don't foam at the mouth, but I do fall down. Sometimes I've attacked people. I did in Montgomery. I was in this hotel and I had this attack and somebody connected with the hotel came to my room and I began to kick him—and that's all I know about that. Then there was an ambulance and all these doctors, but I don't remember any of that. Heavens, what a sensation that caused! Governor Wallace sent me forty-six roses and a message saying could he come and see me. But I was only there for two days. I didn't go on to stay with my aunt. I felt quite undone by the whole thing. I came back to New York and stayed in a hospital for ten days. It leaves you very exhausted.

In 1977 you suffered from a creative and personal crisis: what happened to you then?

I was just trying to do too many things at the same time. I was working on my book *Answered Prayers*; I was doing a film script; I was having an argument with a friend of mine that went on and on endlessly without resolving itself. It was just too many things at the same time and I decided that I'd go to the hospital and have a nice rest.

You've written that this period of your life altered your attitude toward art and writing and truth, so it was an obviously significant time.

Any kind of nervous breakdown, which is what it was, is bound to shift your focus a good deal.

In what ways did it shift your focus?

I became much more objective about my writing. There was a certain distance between me and my work and I could see what I was doing with a far finer, sharper eye. I was also much more objective about myself as a result. I went through several years of psychoanalysis and it did me absolutely no good whatsoever.

Why spend several years at it, then?

It takes about five years to go through a proper analysis.

Was it Freudian?

Yes. It seemed I should at least give it a try, but after going through two years of it, I realized it wasn't doing me any good whatsoever. In fact, I think it was doing me a lot of harm.

Was it affecting your writing?

No, it didn't affect my writing at all. I don't think it really affected anything, that was the trouble with it.

You've written of a point of life saturation, when everything becomes pure effort and total repetition. Do you find yourself drifting in and out of that point or is it something much closer to you?

I think it's drifting in and out. One goes through long periods where you feel like getting up every morning and doing something and then you go through periods where you don't want to get up. I can always tell when I'm going into a depressed state because I don't like to get up, whether I'm asleep or not.

Can you think of living writers who have reached or passed that point of life saturation?

I don't think that anybody can really pass that point, except suicide.

Do you average more than four or five hours of sleep a night?

Just about that.

Do you take catnaps during the day?

No, I can't. I never have been able to nap. Well, once in a while, but it's very unusual. When I swim a lot I can.

In the summer or if I'm in California, I swim every day for about an hour.

You were recently arrested for driving under the influence of alcohol and without a license. The press, naturally, had a field day—especially when you first appeared in court wearing shorts, shocking the judge....

He was lucky I was wearing shoes.

I thought you were wearing sandals.

I *was* wearing sandals.

And was the judge insulted?

Oh yes, he was very insulted that I was taking the whole thing so casually. Actually, I looked quite smart. I had a very smart pair of shorts on and a very smart jacket and shirt and sandals.

This was all thought out?

I never thought about it at all. The photographs—I was on the front page of the *San Francisco Chronicle* across two spreads, across the whole front page; and I looked terrifically smart in *Women's Wear Daily*, which published the picture and said how chic I looked. That was my crime. He never mentioned anything to do with the car or my driver's license or nothing. Everything had to do with the fact I was wearing shorts and sandals.

You didn't wear shorts the second time, though, when you were fined?

I wore a suit. It was very tiresome for such a little tiny nothing, to have thirty photographers sent out from everywhere. *(Laughs.)* There actually is a sign over the courtroom which I hadn't seen. I'd never been there. It says no one is allowed wearing shorts or bare feet or munching jelly peanut sandwiches or whatever.

Didn't your lawyer suggest that you put on a pair of pants?

He suggested that I take off my pants and go to a motel with him! *(Long laugh.)*

Perhaps you should have.

Would have saved the legal fee.

Let's talk about the actual charges. Did you have a license?

I have a license. It just expired.

How long ago?

A couple of months. I would have had my new license except I had to go to an optometrist to have my eye thing put in the thing and I kept putting it off and putting it off. That's really all it was about.

Were you drunk at the time?

No.

Isn't that also what it was about?

I had told a number of people that my license was expired and someone told the police. It was the beginning of the July fourth weekend and they had set up this whole network and they thought, "We'll get Truman Capote." They wanted their names in the papers—and they got their names in the papers. It happened right next to my house, on a perfectly quiet road without another car in sight. There was no accident, I wasn't speeding, I was on my way home for supper. It was still daylight. I had only had two drinks...and I know what I can drink and what I can't. I did the breathalizer test nine times with them, because they couldn't get any registration above .09 the first three times. Then they finally got a reading of .14, which is nothing.

The way it was reported, you said that you didn't think you were drunk, but if they thought so, then you must have been.

No, I didn't say that at all. I said, "Well, that was their opinion." That's all I said.

Do you drink too much at times?

I haven't been drinking hardly at all.

But you do have a couple of drinks a day?

Oh yes, but not every day. And not even every several days. For instance, I haven't had anything to drink before today for like five or six days.

And how many serious bouts have you had with whiskey?

Just that one period from 1976 till 1979.

What about smoking?

I did smoke but I haven't since 1962. I started smoking when I was twelve and I smoked up a chimney.

What about drugs? You've written that you've tried almost everything.

Everything except heroin. But I've given them all up.

Was there any drug that stimulated your imagination?

Cocaine did for a while. I found it a really quite suggestive drug for a period of almost a year, then it started having exactly the opposite effect on me. It used to be I was quite calm but my mind was quite stimulated.

Did you write much on it?

I was writing a lot.

Good material?

Yes, yes. I wrote a lot of *Answered Prayers*. The writing part was good, but suddenly, instead of making me calm, which I need to be—to be physically calm when I write—it made me extremely nervous and it was no good for me. I stopped because of my work—it interfered with my work by making me physically nervous, which is the one thing that I cannot abide.

Were you taking it every day for that year?

Oh yeah.

Was it hard to give up?

No, I gave it up almost at once. I saw that it was not going to work. I had done something and had reached a point with it that maybe most people don't reach, but I had been doing it to excess, I suppose, because I was really using it all the time I was working.

Did it get expensive?

It cost me, that year, about sixty thousand dollars.

What about other drugs? Peyote? Mushrooms?

Yes, but that was so far back when I was a great friend of Aldous Huxley and it never meant anything to me, it was just a little thing I did, just, basically, to please him and Cary Grant. He used to take things with Cary Grant. I had another friend, Virgil Thomson, the composer, who'd been taking these things since he was a child because he came from Arizona where it was quite natural, like high-school kids here smoking marijuana.

What is your feeling about marijuana?

I don't oppose it at all, I think it's fine. I've written that story, "A Day's Work," where I give a perfect description of what I feel using it. But I haven't smoked it in two or three years. I never did smoke it much. One time when I was very young I had a friend who smoked it all the time and I smoked with him. I was about eighteen, this was back in the early forties, long before people were smoking marijuana as an accepted thing, this was such an unaccepted thing then. We used to go to the movies and sit in the balcony, smoking up a storm. Only a few people would turn around and look for a moment. It was fun, we would laugh. I remember smoking all the way through a Bette Davis movie, laughing louder and louder as she got cloudier and cloudier. I just got completely hysterical. The deeper she was drawn into her lover's arms, the funnier I thought it was.

When Studio 54 first started, there was a special little room for friends of the owner where all of the best things were served. I remember smoking marijuana then because I hadn't in a long time and it makes you dance, gives you a terrific looseness. We were smoking Thai sticks and you'd dance for hours.

Do you agree with Proust, that under any rather deep physical pleasure there lies a permanent danger?

Yes, I couldn't agree more. It's the great, serious, one danger in life—'cause if that gets a grip on you, watch out!

In "Mojave" you wrote that certain persons can recognize the truth only when subjected to extreme punishment.

That's true. I can't elaborate on it. It says what it says. Certain people won't admit the truth about themselves or what they'd done until you really put them to the torch.

How true do you think it is that you will die by drowning?

That's what I've been told by several fortune-tellers.

And do you put faith in fortune-tellers?

I've had some very unusual experiences with fortune-tellers. I have to sort of believe in them.

Sort of?

Well, I guess I *do* believe in certain ones. They've been too accurate not to have something very special going for them. There's an amazing fortune-teller here in New York at the moment.

How often do you consult him?

I only consulted him once, but he was really fantastic. He's a curious man. Very expensive. He has this very nice apartment and a secretary and it's like going to see a doctor. His room is like an analyst's room. He asks you, "Please give me something that belongs to you." You give him your wristwatch or a handkerchief or something like that and he holds onto that and then, after a while, he begins to talk and he goes into a trance. He makes a tape recording throughout the entire thing because he says that he doesn't remember what he says once he starts talking. He makes the tape for himself, so that he can play it back and know what he said.

What did he say about you which made you such a believer?

A lot of things. This was three years ago. He doesn't go into the past. It's when they go into the past that I become suspicious of them.

Which is curious, because it's the past you already know.

I know, but they love to linger in the past and I don't care about the past. I want to know about tomorrow. He told me my fortune for about two years and what was going to happen and almost all of it came true.

Did he predict that you would finish Answered Prayers?

Yes.

Missouri, in Other Voices, Other Rooms, *asks Joel: "When you thinks about the Lord, what is it passes in your mind?" What passes in yours?*

That the Lord is everywhere. That God is in everyone. I believed in God very much as a child and then I went through a long period where I didn't believe in God at all. I'm not a newborn Christian, but I came back. As a child, I had to go to church more than any child I can think of. In the South, on Sundays, I went to church three times—morning, midday, and early evening. I went to an Episcopalian school where I had to go to church at eight in the morning, every morning. I know what it is to have had to do all of these things without believing in any of it for a minute. You get down into the real South and you just don't question whether you're religious or not, you just put your money in the plate on Sunday and your place in heaven is already assigned.

Did you really want to escape all that?

Not especially, I like the South.

But did your church experiences make you cynical at an early age?

Not cynical, I just didn't believe in any of it. I was five, six years old and had to go to the Baptist church continuously in Alabama and I just didn't believe any of it. I wrote a short story about this very same subject which my publisher published as *One Christmas.* I originally called it "Why I Believe in Santa Claus." It's one of my best short stories. It's actually based on a true thing in my childhood. I believed in Santa Claus. All my cousins believed in Santa Claus. My old cousin Sook, who was sixty years old, who's in *A Christmas Memory*, she believed in the Lord and Santa Claus and I believed in everything she believed in. I went to New Orleans to spend Christmas with my father and I stayed awake all night and I saw him putting all these presents under the Christmas tree, so I realized there wasn't any Santa Claus. When I went down in the morning, I opened them up and I looked at my father and I said, "Isn't it wonderful, all the things Santa Claus brought me. Now, what are *you* going to give me, Daddy?" *(Laughs at the memory.)*

How did he answer you?

He was in a state of shock.

Earlier, when we talked about abortion, you said you felt women had the right to have them, which goes against church doctrine...

That's the one thing about the Catholic Church... well, there's two things about the Catholic Church.... No, about *seven* things about the Catholic Church that, if it weren't for them, I would be a Catholic, because there's many things about the Catholic Church I do like.

What do you oppose?

Their attitude about abortions is totally unacceptable.

Their attitude about homosexuality is totally unacceptable to me. Their attitude about priests having sex and not having sex is totally unacceptable and ridiculous, it serves no purpose that *I* can see.

Makes for some very strange priests.

Good-bye, I said to Cardinal Cookie, you're out of the closet at last! *(Laughs.)* That son of a bitch hypocrite faggot. Practically every priest I know is gay, anyway. Even the ones that claim they're not, they are. The gay baths in New York, half of the clientele are priests. That's the truth. I was going to do—well, I did do, and I may still put it in—basically a factual thing about gay baths in *Answered Prayers*. One of the characters goes to one. I know several of the people who run most of the gay baths in this country, I've had long conversations with them. There's a gay bath on Columbus Avenue in New York, that doesn't have any signs. There's a door that has no identification at all. Upstairs is one of the most wild gay baths in the western hemisphere. And the man who runs it told me over a third of its clientele are priests.

So, that's three reasons why you don't like the Catholic Church. What about birth control?

That's outrageous, too.

What do *you like about the Church?*

I hate to go to funerals. The only ones I've been to are friends of mine who moved or touched me and they were all Catholics. I think the Catholic ceremonies are really very beautiful. They're marvelous. I went to a funeral of a friend of mine who was a prince of the Catholic Church, where three cardinals were reading the ceremony, which was the most *beautiful* thing. Absolutely fantastic! The choir had about six hundred people . . . and the candles and the incense . . .

What about the belief itself? Can you accept the idea of Christ and the Immaculate Conception?

No. I just like the floor show. *(Laughs.)* It's better than Studio 54.

How do you feel about people's desire for immortality?

Well, I've never had it so I can't tell you. To me, it's the most pointless thing. The only time I even notice it is when I see people with their grandchildren and then I sort of faintly see what it is, why they have such a thing about grandchildren. It has something to do with their concept of immortality.

Do you believe in an afterlife?

I'm not sure.

Do you believe in reincarnation?

I'm not sure.

You don't expect to be a sea turtle in another life?

I said that before, that's because they live to an old, old age and become very wise.

What would you like to come back as?

A buzzard.

Why a buzzard?

Because buzzards are nice and free. Nobody likes them. Nobody cares what they do. You don't have to worry about your friends or your enemies. You're just out there, flapping away, having a good time, looking for something to eat.

Epilogue

Tuesday, August 28, 1984

The cameras were rolling at the entrance to the chapel of the Westwood Village Mortuary. Piano selections from *House of Flowers* were played. The morning memorial was dignified and touching.

Robert Blake, who played Perry Smith in the film of *In Cold Blood*, told how he first met Truman on the set in Kansas. "He taught me more about acting than anyone," Blake said. "He always called me 'Bobby B.' 'Just be yourself, Bobby B. Let it come from inside of you.'"

Blake's fondest memory was of the time Truman once called him from Fire Island, where he had rented a house. There was a hurricane, Blake said, and a dog in labor at the house. "Truman didn't know what to do and I talked him through the delivery. Then Truman dropped the phone and disappeared. When he got back on, he said he was hiding in the kitchen because the dog had tried to bite him. I told him that the dog's natural instinct was to bite the umbilical cord and that he must go back and help. Here I was in Los Angeles, talking to this wonderful, frightened writer as a hurricane shook his house. But he went back and did what he had to."

Armand Deutsch, vice-chairman of the President's Committee on the Arts and Humanities and an old friend of Truman's, spoke next. He told about the party Bennett Cerf threw for Capote when his first novel was published. "It was a very fancy affair and the butler entered, announcing that a boy had come to the door. The boy, of course, was Truman. He loved the party and everyone there was enthralled with him. Bennett Cerf said that after that, Truman never dined at home again."

Alan Schwartz, Truman's lawyer and executor, talked of Capote's wit and his barbs, reserving the former for friends and the latter for his enemies. Then Joanne Carson cried through her reading of the last paragraph from "A Christmas Memory," which she said Truman said was his most perfect work.

Artie Shaw spoke, saying, "Truman died of everything, he died of life, from living a full one. And yet, in his last years, it was as if Truman was ready to give it all up. And in the end, it won't be his celebrity but his work which will be remembered." Shaw went on about the nature of the artist and how Truman was one, which was "so rare. But let us not forget laughter in this time of sadness, because Truman would have liked us to laugh."

A frail, slow-walking Christopher Isherwood was the last to come forward. He said only a few words . . . and then he laughed. And as he laughed, I remembered something Isherwood had said when he spoke to the audience who had come to see his films at that Hollywood theater. Someone had asked him how he felt about getting older. "If age came walking through that door, one would turn and run," he avowed. "But it seeps up so nicely."

So had death seeped up on Truman.

The song "Don't Like Goodbyes," was sung as people stood to pay their last respects. As I stood before the closed coffin, I put my hand on the richly stained wood and whispered goodbye. Truman's words suddenly floated inside my head. It was his response to the reaction of some of those he had thinly disguised in the published chapters of *Answered Prayers*.

"I can't understand why everybody's so upset," he said. "What do they think they had around them, a court jester? They had a writer."

Selected Bibliography

Books by Truman Capote

Other Voices, Other Rooms, New York: Random House, 1948.
Tree of Night and other Stories, New York: Random House, 1949.
Local Color, New York: Random House, 1950.
The Grass Harp, New York: Random House, 1951.
The Grass Harp, (play), New York: Random House, 1952.
The Muses Are Heard, New York: Random House, 1956.
A Christmas Memory, New York: Random House, 1956.
Breakfast at Tiffany's, a Novella and Three Stories (including "House of Flowers," "A Diamond Guitar," "A Christmas Memory"), New York: Random House, 1958.
Observations (Photographs by Richard Avedon, comments by Truman Capote), New York: Simon and Schuster, 1959.
Selected Writings of Truman Capote, New York: Random House, 1963.
In Cold Blood, New York: Random House, 1965.
A Thanksgiving Visitor, New York: Random House, 1967.
Trilogy (an experiment in multimedia, the personal story of the making of a film & the original Capote stories and the script. By Truman Capote, Eleanor and Frank Perry. The stories include: "A Christmas Memory," "Miriam," and "Among the Paths to Eden"), New York: The Macmillan Company, 1969.

The Dogs Bark: Public People & Private Places, New York: Random House, 1973.
Answered Prayers, (excerpts):
"Mojave," *Esquire* Magazine, June, 1975.
"La Côte Basque, 1965," *Esquire* Magazine, November, 1975.
"Unspoiled Monsters," *Esquire* Magazine, May, 1976.
"Kate McCloud," *Esquire* Magazine, December, 1976.
Music for Chameleons, New York: Random House, 1980.
One Christmas, New York: Random House, 1983.

FILMS (IN COLLABORATION)

Stazione Termini/Indiscretion of an American Wife (dialogue only), Italy, 1953.
Beat the Devil, UK/Italy, 1954.
The Innocents, UK/US, 1961.
Trilogy (from three of his short stories; originally shown on TV), 1969.

Index